Adaptive Snowsports Instruction

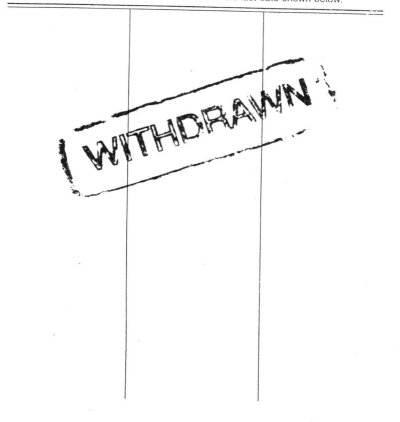

Credits

EDUCATION DIRECTOR
Linda J. Crockett

EDITING
ABC Editing Ink

PRODUCTION MANAGEMENT
Rebecca W. Ayers

DESIGN & PRODUCTION
EnZed Design

ILLUSTRATIONS
Greg Grigoriou

PRINTING & PREPRESS
American Web, Inc.
GraphX, Inc.
Sprint Press, Inc.

Table of Contents

Acknowledgments

Contributors

Two people were instrumental in getting this book to press. Gwen Allard, who served as the National Adaptive Committee Chair for PSIA-AASI (Professional Ski Instructors of America–American Association of Snowboard Instructors) from 1996 to 2002, orchestrated the group effort to provide this new text. What started out as a revision of the *Adaptive Manual* (PSIA 1996) eventually expanded to become this new book under Gwen's guidance. Neil Lundberg, member of the PSIA-AASI National Adaptive Committee, sifted through the compilation of material provided by the committee members and their colleagues, working as lead author to shape the material into a cohesive whole as it now appears. Both of these individuals went above and beyond the call of duty in advancing adaptive snowsports.

The authors of this manuscript provide a truly impressive depth of talent and experience. Their expertise, ability to communicate, and willingness to share is indispensible to PSIA-AASI adaptive programs, and they are a tribute to their profession. The contributing authors are listed here.

- Lead Author: Neil Lundberg
- Chapter 1: Theresa Day and Robert Harney, M.D.
- Chapter 2: Frank Williamson
- Chapter 3: Kathy Chandler and Theresa Day
- Chapter 4: Sherrie Nevill
- Chapter 5: Neil Lundberg and Will Rahill
- Chapter 6: Peter Axelson
- Chapter 7: Dave Henderson
- Chapter 8: Beth Fox

- Chapter 9: Peter Axelson and Will Rahill
- Chapter 10: Neil Lundberg, Will Rahill, and Paul Speight
- Chapter 11: Bill Bowness
- Chapter 12: Karen Frei, Bobby Palm, Earl Saline, and Frank Williamson
- Chapter 13: Gwen Allard, Michael Byxbe, Candace Cable, Betsy Doyon, Jon Kreamelmeyer, Neil Lundberg, and Mickey Stone
- Chapter 14: Peter Axelson
- References: John Stevenson

PSIA and AASI gratefully acknowledge those who reviewed this manuscript and offered their valuable suggestions. Reviewers for this book include: Gwen Allard, Bill Bowness, Theresa Day, Beth Fox, Karen Frei, Kevin Jardine, Neil Lundberg, Mike Milter, John Swartwood, and Karen Witt.

Many adaptive skiers, snowboarders, and instructors gave freely of their time to serve as models for our photos. This talent pool included members of the U.S. Disabled Ski Team. Our models were: Tommy Banks, Michael Byxbe, Jeff J. Cain, M.D., Pat Carr, Paul Combs, Billie Cornell, Bruce Cornell, Muffy Davis, Beth Fox, Adam Fromma, Quintin Gray, Jan Hess, Duncan Hillery, Daniel Kosick, Nancy Clair Laird, Haakon Lang-Ree, Dave Littman, Neil Lundberg, Bobby McMullen, Aaron A. Norman, Judy Over, Mary Riddell, Jacob E. Rife, Katherine Hays Rodriguez, Earl Saline, George Sansonetis, Joseph Tompkins, Karen Witt, and Christopher Devlin Young.

Foreword

Brian W. Robb

Welcome! Since you are beginning to delve into the PSIA-AASI *Adaptive Snowsports Instruction* manual, it is likely that you are among the select few who not only have an unquenchable love of skiing and snowboarding and a desire to share your enthusiasm and skills with others, but who also have the courage and commitment to tackle perhaps the greatest challenge of any snowsports instructors—bringing the thrill of mountains in winter and of gliding down powder-covered slopes, mastering gravity instead of being mastered by it.

Throughout this manual, we use the terms "instructor" and "student" because this is the most common situation and fits with the usage in other PSIA and AASI technical manuals. However, the reality is much different. Often, the people with whom you will share all or part of your day at the slopes will already have impressive physical skills and unbridled courage. What they may lack, however, is the ability to ski or snowboard alone or to use standard "off-the-shelf" equipment. In these cases, you are not so much an instructor as a guide, and they are less students than guests, clients, and partners.

Just as often, you will find that *you* are the student. Your key to success, and that of your students or guests, is to treat each lesson as an opportunity to learn about the person and the disability, how best to build confidence and understanding, and what combinations of teaching tools and progressions can most effectively lead to the common goals of fun, safety, and realistic skill development.

We hope that reading and studying the following material will get you started by providing basic information on the adaptations necessary to teach students with disabilities. This manual represents years of experience and the hard work of hundreds of instructors and snowsports enthusiasts. Special thanks go to those who contributed their time, energy, and skills to bring forth this knowledge. We hope you enjoy reading and studying this manual; we know you will have fun and find fulfillment in teaching adaptive skiers and riders!

Introducing Adaptive Skiing and Riding

This manual describes the types of disabilities you are likely to encounter and the specific types of equipment, other tools, and teaching approaches best suited to each situation. It addresses cognitive and developmental disabilities, visual or hearing impairments, and other physical disabilities through adaptive skiing and riding techniques that evolved to meet unique needs—i.e., four-track and three-track stand-up skiing, sit-down skiing using mono-ski or bi-ski devices, and specialized snowboarding and nordic equipment. Other adaptive disciplines are emerging and undoubtedly will be addressed in future manuals.

What You Will Not Find in this Manual

This manual was not designed as a stand-alone source of information but was developed in conjunction with other educational material produced by PSIA and AASI. The current educational concept of PSIA-AASI is to reduce duplication of material while striving for consistency among snowsports instructors in areas common to all.

The adaptive, alpine, nordic, and snowboarding manuals describe discipline-specific tools and techniques that build upon the *Core Concepts for Snowsports Instructors Manual* (PSIA 2001). The first edition of the *Adaptive Manual* (PSIA 1997) contained considerable material relating to the process of teaching a lesson. Updated information

relating to teaching is contained in the *Core Concepts* manual and a variety of other snowsports materials.

Adaptive instructors currently rely most heavily on information and equipment for the alpine discipline. Some adaptive snowboarding and nordic information is also presented in this manual.

Because of our close tie to the alpine discipline, adaptive instructors need to have a working knowledge of the *Alpine Technical Manual* (PSIA 2002). For practical purposes, the alpine material has not been comprehensively included in this manual but should be part of every adaptive instructor's library.

Etiquette and Responsibility

Skiing and snowboarding involve moving at high speeds down a sometimes steep and narrow hill. They are a constant attempt to avoid obstacles, including people, trees, rocks, snowcats, lift towers, varied snow conditions, or other obstacles. "By its very nature, skiing is an inherently risky sport, and anyone who chooses to ski must accept this inherent risk" (*Alpine Manual*, PSIA 1996).

As a teacher, it is your job to maintain a professional attitude, be a role model to everyone who interacts with you on the mountain, and help others be aware of risks. You have a distinct advantage in knowing the mountain, the terrain, and the snow conditions du jour, as well as knowing where it is wise and unwise to ski or board relative to your students' abilities. Make a point of sharing this knowledge with your students and peers daily.

ETIQUETTE

Have you ever been somewhere unfamiliar and had your day "made" by an encounter with a really helpful and courteous person? An enjoyable time on the slopes does not only come from good weather and great snow conditions. A fun day does not only happen because your equipment is tuned properly and your boots feel good. You can make somebody's day by simply being polite, respectful, and willing to take the time to listen and help others get what they need. As a teacher, you are an ambassador for your sport, your ski area, your resort's learning center, and your peers. You should always strive to be:

- Professional
- Responsible
- Accountable
- Ethical
- Risk aware
- A role model
- A mentor
- A source of information
- A source of inspiration

Enthusiasm is contagious. Let your passion for the sport create new, committed participants. Remember, everybody at the resort is a guest.

Whether dealing with tuners in the shop, peers in the learning center, employees from other parts of the mountain, or the students themselves, you have an opportunity to make a difference in everybody's day. Be the first one to make contact. Make a point of learning and remembering names. Be concerned about the welfare of others. Treat coworkers and peers with the same respect and courtesy as your guests. Live the quality of life you love by demonstrating your passions through your actions.

RESPONSIBILITY

People who come to the slopes are looking for a carefree, injury free, and hassle-free day. The industry has adopted a code called Your Responsibility Code that allows you and others to help create a responsible and enjoyable experience on the mountain. It is important that you know this code and you share it with others. However, as an ambassador for snowsports, it is even more important that you live the code every day that you are on the slopes.

Your Responsibility Code

1. Always stay in control.
2. People ahead of you have the right of way.
3. Stop in a safe place for you and others.
4. Whenever starting downhill or merging, look uphill and yield.
5. Use devices to help prevent runaway equipment.
6. Observe signs and warning, and keep off closed trails.
7. Know how to use the lifts safely.

Know the code. It's your responsibility.

OTHER GUIDELINES FOR FUN AND SAFE SKIING AND SNOWBOARDING

Body Basics

- Apply at least 15 SPF broad-spectrum sunscreen, whether the day is sunny or cloudy.
- Drink water frequently to avoid the dehydrating effects of altitude.
- Layer with breathable, water-wicking layers that can be added or subtracted with changes in the weather.

Serious Signage

- Green Circle: Easiest trails and more mellow slopes.
- Blue Square: More difficult trails and intermediate slopes.
- Black Diamond: Most difficult trails and steep or bumped slopes.
- Double Black Diamond: Experts only.
- Caution Triangle: Heads up, this terrain may contain hazards.
- Red Octagon with Slash through Skier: Trail or area is closed. No skiing allowed.

Learn Your Limits

- Avoid taking that one last run when you are feeling overly fatigued.
- Ski and ride at your own level. Test your skills to improve, but know when you're crossing over into dangerous territory. (Patrollers say this is the number one safety issue at resorts.)
- Control your speed. Respect others on the mountain, especially in high-traffic areas where trails are merging.

Reinforce Your Responsibility Code throughout the lesson and the day.

ADDITIONAL VARIABLES FOR A GREAT LESSON

Risk awareness, risk management, and a great lesson involve more than the responsibility code and a professional attitude. A well-managed lesson takes into account other variables. Below are other things to consider that will help make each ski lesson a more enjoyable and valuable experience:

■ Check to see if students have equipment and clothing that fits and is appropriate for the conditions. If any students do not have the correct equipment or clothing for the day, escort or direct them to a shop where they can be properly outfitted.

■ Take the students to terrain that is appropriate and suitable for their ability level to avoid unnecessary risks.

■ Be aware of the students' level of conditioning and level of fatigue.

■ Be mindful of the lowest level of skiing and the slowest skiers in your group. Make sure they receive adequate instruction on appropriate terrain.

■ Take constant note of the snow conditions and terrain variations. Use this knowledge to help your students have a better experience.

■ Keep a close eye on the weather and alert the students to changes. The students have other things on their minds, and bad weather can hinder learning and fun.

■ Be familiar with the mountains you are skiing: being a bit of a tour guide adds intrigue to the lesson.

■ Keep the students on a steady pace and well hydrated. High altitudes and mountain weather can deplete people of essential energy.

■ Be familiar with emergency phone locations, phone numbers, and your resort's emergency procedures so that any accidents may be dealt with efficiently and professionally.

■ Have knowledge of the town—the shops, restaurants, the night life, etc. Your students will elicit *all* your expertise, not just that which pertains to snowsports.

Being a professional requires more than following the suggestions listed here. A true professional constantly searches for ways to grow. See the *Core Concepts* manual for more information on etiquette and responsibility.

Brian W. Robb

Disability Awareness and Medical Terminology

chapter 1

Adaptive snowsports programs work with a wide range of disabled people to provide the unique exhilaration of this sport. To be truly effective, the adaptive snowsports instructor must be versatile and knowledgeable about disabilities so that the experience can be both safe and fun. This chapter describes some of the more common disabilities among students as well as medications they may use.

Specific questions about certain medications can be researched in the *Physician's Desk Reference* (PDR) or similar text, which are useful to keep in the snowsports room.

PHOTO 1.1 Skier with Above-knee Amputation

Brian W. Robb

The Disabilities
AMPUTATION OR LIMB DEFICIENCY

Limb deficiency may be congenital, traumatic, or the result of disease (e.g., diabetes, which may cause vascular insufficiency leading to amputation).

The level (position on the body) of amputation will determine which adaptive method the student will choose. Some students use their prostheses, while others do not. This decision is ultimately left to the student, but at times the instructor may need to educate the athlete as to what does nor does not work.

Deficiencies in the upper extremities include:

- shoulder disarticulation (no arm below the shoulder socket)
- above-elbow amputation (AEA)
- below elbow amputation (BEA)

Deficiencies in the lower extremities include:

- **sacral agenesis**—lack of development, in which the lower pelvis and legs never form
- **hemipelvectomy**— in which half of the pelvis and the associated leg are gone
- **above-knee amputation (AKA)**—prostheses usually not used for skiing or riding
- **below-knee amputation (BKA)**—prostheses optional while skiing or riding

Medications used by limb-deficient patients may include insulin (for people with diabetes) or blood thinners such as Coumadin to prevent clotting.

Special considerations for these students include the following:

- If the student chooses to wear a prosthesis, be sure it is secured properly to the limb to avoid friction injuries or unwanted movement. If the student has an arm or hand prosthesis consisting of a hook, the prosthesis should be covered to protect the student and others.
- Prosthetic design and technology have improved greatly over the years, and some of the advanced snowsports athletes use a "ski leg" that positions the limb in a more efficient manner for skiing or snowboarding.
- Coumadin can cause excessive bleeding, either internally or externally, from a fall.
- Since many amputations are caused by vascular disease, the student may be hypersensitive to cold. Be sure to protect the stump and watch for frostbite.

SPINAL CORD INJURY

The spinal column is a protective tube of bone (vertebrae) that protects the nerve tissue known as the spinal cord. The spinal cord is an electrical network that in effect is an "extension cord" from the brain and that controls the neuromuscular activity of the body. Injury or damage to the cord may cause complete or incomplete paralysis at or below the level of injury, including:

- **Quadriplegia**—paralysis from the neck down
- **Quadriparesis**—partial paralysis from the neck down
- **Paraplegia**—paralysis of the lower extremities
- **Paraparesis**—partial paralysis of the lower extremities

Anatomy of the Spine

The spine consists of:

- seven cervical (neck) vertebrae (eight nerves)
- twelve thoracic (upper back) vertebrae
- five lumbar (mid-back) vertebrae
- five sacral (lower back) vertebrae (fused)
- one coccyx ("tail bone")

Table 1 presents a summary of the muscles or muscle groups innervated (controlled) by nerves at the various vertebral levels and the functions of those muscles.

Level of Injury

The most common levels of injury to the spinal cord are C5-6, T6-7, and T12-L1. Paralysis may be complete or incomplete. For example, complete T6 paraplegia consists of loss of motor and sensory function below the sixth thoracic vertebra, while incomplete T6 paraplegia involves some retained motor and sensory function below this level.

Functional Levels

The functional level is determined by the level ("height") of the injury. As a general rule, a person with a T6 or higher injury will use a bi-ski; T6 to L5 will probably use a mono-ski; and L5 or below will probably be a stand-up skier (e.g., four-track).

Special considerations for these types of disabilities include:

- **Autonomic dysreflexia**—Common with T6 or higher injuries, this is an involuntary response of the autonomic nervous system to caustic stimuli (bladder/bowel distention, pressure sores, severe cold/heat, injury) and is a life-threatening, hypertensive crisis produced by the body's inability to sense and react to these stimuli. The symptoms may include a panicky feeling of "impending doom," flushing of the skin, headache, sweating, blurred vision, or a sudden change in the ability to communicate or comprehend. Though students who have experienced it know the symptoms and will warn you, if you ever suspect this syndrome, make sure all straps are loosened around any indwelling catheter and that it is free of kinks, get into a warm place, call the ski patrol, and seek first aid immediately. This is a medical emergency.
- **Spinal fusion**—Common among students who have had spinal injuries, this surgery fuses vertebrae to stiffen the spine, often supported by metal rods, clamps, or hooks. The supports may be prominent under the skin and should be padded or protected.

TABLE 1.1 Spinal Nerves and Muscle Functions

Spinal Nerves	Muscles Innervated	Function
C1–C2	Upper neck muscles	Aid in head control
C3–C4	Diaphragm	Inhalation
C5–C6	Deltoids	Shoulder flexion, abduction
	Biceps	Elbow flexion
C6–C7	Extensor carpi radialis	Wrist dorsiflexion
	Pronator teres	Wrist pronation
C7–C8	Triceps	Elbow extension
	Extensor digitorum communis	Finger extension
C8, T1	Flexor digitorum superficialis	Finger flexion
	Opponens pollicis	Thumb opposition
	Interossei	Spreading and closing fingers
T2–T6	Intercostals	Forced inhalation
T6–T12	Intercostals	Exhalation
	Abdominals	Aid in forced expiration (coughing) and trunk flexion
L1–L3	Iliopsoas hip flexion	Adductors Hip Adduction
L3, L4	Quadriceps	Knee extension
L4–L5, S1	Gluteus medius	Hip abduction
	Tibialis anterior	Foot dorsiflexion (bringing foot up)
L5, S1–S2	Gluteus maximus	Hip extension
	Gastrocnemius	Plantar flexion of the foot (walking on toes)
S2–S4	Anal sphincter	Bowel control
	Urethral sphincter	Bladder control

Be aware that these rods supports may extend for along a good portion of the spine and may inhibit its normal flexion and extension.

- **Thermoregulation**—The ability to regulate body temperature may be altered in students with spinal cord injury, especially at or above the T8 level. Paralyzed limbs have reduced circulatory flow, so wearing warm, dry clothing on the extremities is important to minimize chill. Circulatory checks should be made regularly.

NEUROMUSCULAR DISEASES

Spina Bifida

A congenital abnormality in which the spinal column does not close completely around the spinal cord, usually at the L5-S1 level. The diagnosis is commonly made as a result of bowel and bladder incontinence, clubbed feet, or congenital hip dislocation. Other symptoms range from mild muscle imbalance and sensory loss to complete paraplegia.

A child born with a **meningocele** (in which the meninges or spinal covering bulges through the defect in the spinal column) usually has little or no neurological deficit because the spinal cord itself remains within the canal.

A child born with a **meningomyelocele** (the spinal cord bulges through the defect in the spinal column) has neurological deficit, including bladder and bowel incontinence and, in about half the cases, hydrocephalus (increased pressure in the ventricles of the brain due to cerebrospinal fluid, or CSF).

For centuries, children died of sepsis (general infection), urinary tract infections, meningitis, and hydrocephalus. Today, antibiotics control infection and surgery is used to correct the structural defect.

Special considerations for *spina bifida* include:

- **Urinary tract infections**—Medications include Bactrim, Septra, Macrodantin, and ciprofloxin.
- **Bladder spasms**—Medications include Urecholine, Ditropan, and Daricon.
- **Bladder care**—Students may have an indwelling catheter (a tube inserted into the bladder and connected to a plastic bag that collects the urine, known as a "leg bag"). When using a bi-ski or mono-ski, it is important to ensure that straps or other aspects of the equipment do not restrict flow in the catheter.
- **Allergic reactions**—Many students will be allergic to latex. A low-grade allergy may appear in the form of a skin rash (urticaria) or itching (pruritus). A high-grade allergic reaction may take the form of seizures or anaphylactic shock, which can be life-threatening.

Cerebral Palsy

Cerebral palsy (CP) is a disorder of movement or posture resulting from damage to the immature brain and is not genetic. It usually results from oxygen deficit but can also be caused by trauma to the brain.

Damage can be:

- **Prenatal**—infection, anoxia, placenta pathology, toxemia, Rh factor incompatibility, metabolic disturbances
- **Natal**—anoxia, hemorrhage, prolapsed cord, trauma, prematurity, congenital anemia
- **Postnatal**—brain contusion, skull fractures, infections, vascular problems, anoxia, common respiratory distress syndrome

Effects on extremities may involve:

- **Quadriplegia**—all four limbs
- **Diplegia**—all four limbs, but with mild involvement of the upper extremities
- **Paraplegia**—lower extremities
- **Monoplegia**—only one extremity
- **Hemiplegia**—one side of the body
- **Triplegia**—three extremities

The three main types of CP are:

- **Spastic**—The most common type, involves spastic contraction of the extremities with tense muscles, usually in flexion.
- **Athetoid**—Involuntary, purposeless movements with flailing of the extremities or trunk. Movements are described as extraneous or uncontrolled.
- **Ataxic**—Jerky, uncontrolled movements that cause the person to appear clumsy or uncoordinated. Balance is severely affected, but muscle tone is normal.

The student with CP may appear rigid (with stiff, uncontrolled movements) or flaccid (with low muscle tone) and exhibit other characteristics such as bladder or bowel incontinence, scoliosis (laterally curved spine), visual impairment, altered speech patterns, fatigue due to the excessive energy needed to overcome the lack of autonomic control, and mental retardation. Be careful not to assume mental retardation, however.

Depending on the nature and extent of the disability, people with CP may require physical therapy, occupational therapy, communication therapy, orthopedic management, and bracing. Medications may consist of tranquilizers and antispasm compounds (Valium, Robaxin, Flexeril, etc.).

Special considerations in snowsports instruction include the following:

- For mild CP, two-track skiing is usually possible.
- Hemiplegia may work with either two-track or four-track skiing and require either on one pole or one outrigger.
- Paraplegia may work with two-track, four-track, bi-ski, or mono-ski equipment.
- Diplegia, quadriplegia, or triplegia normally require a mono-ski or bi-ski.
- A variety of braces are used. See the discussion for post-polio on this page.

Spino-cerebellar Degeneration
Spino-cerebellar degeneration is characterized by breakdown of the ascending and descending tracks in the spinal cord at different levels. The two main types are:

- **Charcot-Marie-Tooth Disease**— Also known as peroneal muscular atrophy disease, this condition afflicts the peroneal muscles along the outer side of the lower leg that control pronation and plantar flexion of the foot. This is an inherited condition and is more common in boys than in girls. The disease manifests itself in late childhood or early adulthood and is characterized by high arches and muscle atrophy of the peroneals and toe extensors. The upper arm may also be involved. The disease is usually permanent, and the student is usually ambulatory using an ankle-foot orthosis (ASO) brace.
- **Friedreich's Ataxia**—This condition involves degeneration of the posterior and lateral tracks of the spinal cord and cerebellum. This results in loss of position sense,

poor balance, and ataxia. This is also an inherited disorder and it occurs in early childhood with the development of high arches (*pes cavus*) and claw toes. The student shows cerebellar ataxia, which displays itself as swaying with a staggering or irregular gait. The degeneration is progressive, and many times the student will become wheelchair-dependent. Cardiac disease may cause premature death.

Multiple Sclerosis
Multiple sclerosis (MS) is a neurological disability in which the body's nerve fibers degenerate and become scarred or sclerosed. This scarring can take place at multiple locations throughout the nervous system, hence the name. The scarring blocks electrical pulses along the nerve, resulting in a variety of symptoms. Characteristic of MS is its cyclic exacerbation and remission (worsening and lessening). The individual may be quite strong and coordinated one day, but weak and unbalanced the next. Students with MS may experience paralysis or weakness of their extremities, an associated loss of stamina, and poor balance. Some visual impairment may also be present, as well as a tendency for mood swings with no apparent cause (laughing one moment and crying the next). As the disease progresses, slurred speech and incontinence may develop. Students with MS may have trouble processing information and organizing thoughts.

When teaching someone with MS, be aware of potential fatigue and varying ability from day to day.

Muscular Dystrophy
Muscular dystrophy (MD) includes several different disorders that cause progressive and irreversible wasting of muscle tissue. Most types are hereditary. Degeneration originates within the muscle tissue itself, as opposed to other disorders in which atrophy results from a neurological anomaly (e.g., MS). Voluntary and involuntary muscle functions are likely to be involved. Although MD comprises approximately nine diseases, the two most common are:

- **Myotonic MD**—usually begins between ages 20 and 40 and is slowly progressive, affecting the central nervous system, eyes, heart, and endocrine glands.
- **Duchenne MD**—usually begins between ages 2 and 6 and is often fatal due to respiratory depression.

Although students with MD may ambulate with the aid of crutches or a cane, they will eventually be wheelchair-dependent. Be aware that poor muscle strength and a tendency to tire easily increase the risk of injury.

Post-polio Syndrome
Post-polio syndrome refers to the lingering effects of poliomyelitis, a viral infection of the spinal cord. This may cause paralysis in either the respiratory/trunk muscles or the leg muscles. Paralysis is permanent, and the residual effects upon the respiratory/trunk muscles may cause fatigue, shortness of breath, and problems with balance. Some of these may develop years after the initial paralysis. Circulation problems and susceptibility to cold may also occur.

CEREBROVASCULAR ACCIDENT (STROKE) AND TRAUMATIC BRAIN INJURY

Cardiovascular accident (CVA), or stroke, and traumatic brain injury (TBI) describe a sudden weakness or other neurological symptoms caused by an injury to a blood vessel in the brain. The location of the injury in the brain determines what type of symptom results, and where the symptom is expressed. Damage on one side of the brain affects the opposite side of the body.

Organic causes may include death of brain tissue due to hemorrhage (leakage or rupture), aneurysm (ballooning), embolism (clotting), or occlusion (e.g., by plaque deposits) of a blood vessel that deprives oxygen or creates excessive pressure.

Inorganic causes may include damage resulting from an invasive injury such as a gunshot or non-invasive injury such as automobile accident or fall.

The brain is the source of virtually all voluntary and involuntary activities of ordinary life, including autonomic body functions, voluntary and involuntary movements, thought, and emotion. Depending on the portion of the brain affected, the individual may be minimally or profoundly disabled, and symptoms may be physiological or cognitive in nature.

A common aspect of CVA or TBI is hemiplegia or hemiparesis—a complete or partial loss, respectively, of function or control of one side of the body. This lack of bilaterality makes it difficult to balance and hence to ski standing up. Another symptom of hemiplegia may be that of aversion to the affected side of the body, in which objects on that side are not seen or ignored, creating the risk of collision.

Visual deficits may include double vision, reduced depth perception, and diminished spatial orientation.

Both emotional and psychosocial behavior may also be affected. The student may suddenly laugh, cry, or exhibit anger with no appropriate stimulus. Low frustration tolerance in some may cause explosive outbursts when a task cannot be executed or communication understood. Loss of impulse control may give rise to inappropriate comments or aggressive actions. In such a case, the instructor should be reasonably assertive and set limits.

A CVA or TBI student may also experience short-term or long-term memory loss. Any comment or instructions may be acted on initially but forgotten entirely before the next run or lesson. **Aphasia**, the inability to understand words and their meanings, may prevent a student from speaking words formulated in the mind (expressive aphasia) or understanding words when heard (receptive aphasia). **Dysarthria** is a speech deficit in which the language-producing muscles do not work, resulting in garbled, incomprehensible sounds—although the speaker may be unaware of it. The instructor should feel comfortable repeating instructions and ask yes or no questions based on the context of what is happening in the lesson. In some cases, you may need to ask the student to express the thought using different words.

Some CVA or TBI students may be predisposed to seizures. Since the brain is a complex assemblage of electrical connections, disruption of the normal processes can "short circuit" the neural impulses. Seizures may simply be nonconvulsive, with momentary loss of attention or a distant gaze, or characterized by violent, full-body tremors, loss of bladder or bowel control, loss of consciousness, and shallow breathing. While these typically pass in a matter of minutes, they may leave the student exhausted and in need of a rest. Instructors should be aware of a student's predisposition to seizures, especially when riding a chair lift.

DIABETES

Diabetes is a disease in which the pancreas is unable to secrete the appropriate amount of insulin to control blood sugar. The two types of diabetes are **juvenile (Type 1)**, which occurs early in life, and **adult onset (Type 2)**, which occurs later in life. Depending on the type of diabetes, the blood sugar needs to be controlled by diet, oral insulin, or injected insulin.

Special considerations when teaching diabetics include:

- **Diabetic shock**—Occurs when blood sugar increases to such an extent that coma results. Treatment includes injection of insulin, administered by medical personnel.
- **Insulin shock**—Occurs when blood sugar falls to an extremely low level from over-exercise or an over-supply of insulin. Treatment includes ingestion of sugar and evaluation by medical personnel.

Both of these conditions may be characterized by symptoms such as weakness, dizziness, and loss of coordination before onset of a seizure or coma.

Complications

As diabetes progresses, and especially if it is uncontrolled, complications can develop. Vascular problems with microcirculation (capillary flow) may lead to hypothermia and, potentially, amputation as a result of tissue death (necrosis). Eye problems may include macular degeneration and diabetic retinopathy.

VISUAL IMPAIRMENT

Visual impairment is most often described in terms of acuity and range. The legal definition of blindness is a corrected visual acuity of 20/200 or less, or a peripheral field restriction to a diameter of 20° or less, in the better eye. Thus, a person who is legally blind may be able to discern objects only at close distances or have vision limited to a small field of view (like looking through a narrow tube). Since more than 90 percent of people who are legally blind have some residual eyesight, it is important to determine the amount of vision your student has and ensure that your teaching strategy takes full advantage of any residual vision.

Common types and causes of visual impairments are as follows.

- **Retinitis pigmentosa (RP)** is a progressive hereditary disorder that usually appears in childhood and causes slow degeneration of the light receptors in both eyes. The rods (for black-and-white vision) are affected most, usually resulting in night blindness. Peripheral vision decreases progressively, leading to "tunnel vision." No satisfactory treatment for this disease is currently available.

- **Glaucoma** is one of the leading causes of blindness in the United States. It occurs when the fluid inside the forward part of the eye fails to drain properly, thereby causing an increase in intraocular pressure. This eventually causes nerve damage and loss of vision. It is more common in adults over the age of 40. The initial symptoms are a blurred or foggy vision, with eventual loss of vision. Those at risk of developing chronic glaucoma are people over the age of 35 who have had diabetes, myopia, or a family history of glaucoma. The treatment is somewhat limited, and includes eyedrops for early forms of glaucoma, and occasionally surgery may be effective.

- **Cataracts** are opaque or clouded areas on the lens that block passage of light into the eye. Initial symptoms include blurred or double vision and sensitivity to light. The likelihood of developing cataracts increases with age, but the condition can also be hereditary, congenital, or caused by chemical burns. Treatment consists of surgery.

- **Detached retina** is a condition in which the retina, which contains the light-receiving rods and cones, becomes separated from the back of the eye. Although the detachment is painless, it results in loss of vision in the detached area and can cause total blindness of the affected eye if severe. Treatment consists of surgery to reattach the retina.

- **Macular degeneration** is a progressive disease that affects the central part of the retina, known as the macula. Although more common in the elderly, macular degeneration can occur at any age, resulting in loss of vision in the center of the field of view that gradually worsens. Treatment options are limited, and surgery is used to halt the disease from progressing.

- **Optic nerve disease** ranges from a mild loss of acuity to an enlarged blind spot or total loss of vision. Causes include congenital disease, multiple sclerosis (most common), tumors, glaucoma, high blood pressure, diabetes, nutritional deficiencies, or chemical poisoning.

- **Diabetic retinopathy** is visual impairment caused by a weakening of the lining of the blood vessels in the eye. This causes hemorrhage and scarring on the retina. This tissue then contracts and pulls the retina away from the back of the eye. The degree of retinopathy seems more related to the duration of the diabetes than its stability (that is, control of blood sugar). It usually occurs after the person has had diabetes for 10 years or more.

DEVELOPMENTAL AND COGNITIVE DISABILITIES

By definition, a developmental disability is a condition resulting from congenital abnormalities, trauma, disease, or deprivation that interrupts or delays normal fetal, infantile, or juvenile growth and development. The onset is before age 18, and duration is indefinite (i.e., persisting throughout the remaining lifespan). Some of the more common conditions include mental retardation, cerebral palsy, autism, epilepsy, and Down's syndrome.

A cognitive disability consists of damage to, or deterioration of, any portion of the brain that affects the ability to process information, coordinate and control the body, or move in space. Cognitive disabilities are classified as either organic (related to disease such as Alzheimer's, Parkinson's, Huntington's, brain tumors, cerebrovascular disease) or non-organic (caused by injury or trauma, such as traumatic brain injury).

Mental Retardation

Mental retardation (MR) refers to subnormal intellectual ability present from birth or early infancy, manifested by abnormal development and associated with difficulties in learning and social adaptation. This disability constitutes the largest percentage of all people with developmental disabilities. More than 250 specific causes have been identified and grouped into two main categories: medical (hereditary, prenatal, trauma to mother/infant) and social (lack of mental stimulation, physical abuse, poverty).

A classification system has been developed to describe MR based on the person's mental ability (IQ), social behavior (social quotient), and rate of infantile physical development. The four levels and their relative percentage of MR individuals are:

- **Mild**—IQ between 51 and 70 (89 percent); capable of learning academic and prevocational skills with some special training.
- **Moderate**—IQ between 36 and 50 (6 percent); capable of learning academic skills during school age and can be independent in familiar surroundings. Can perform semi-skilled work and function in community homes as adults.

- **Severe**—IQ between 21 and 35 (3.5 percent); physical disabilities such as visual deficiencies or motor dysfunction are common. May have limited communication skills but are able to care for personal needs. As adults, are able to contribute to self-maintenance in work and living situations with supervision.
- **Profound**—IQ of 20 or less (1.5 percent); show minimal responsiveness and may have physical disabilities. Self-care skills and communication may be somewhat limited. As adults, can attend to basic needs and perform work activities that are highly structured.

The leading types of abnormalities or other causes of MR are:

- **Prenatal**—genetic factors, congenital infections, drugs, chemical agents, radiation
- **Postnatal**—viral infections, bacterial infections, lead or mercury poisoning, head injury, asphyxia (e.g., partial drowning)
- **Chromosomal**—Down's syndrome, Fragile X syndrome, Klinefelter's syndrome, Turner's syndrome, Hunter's syndrome, Tay-Sachs disease, and many others
- **Genetic neurological**—tuberous sclerosis, neurofibromatosis, myotonic dystrophy
- **Congenital infection**—rubella virus/measles and cytomegalovirus

Down's Syndrome

Down's syndrome (trisomy 21) is the result of having three of chromosome 21, instead of the usual two of each chromosome (one from the father and one from the mother; human beings have 46 chromosomes, or 23 chromosome pairs).

Down's syndrome causes mild to severe retardation in 100 percent of the cases. It occurs in one of every 660 newborns, making it the most common malformation in human embryos that survive to birth.

Common characteristics include a flat face, a short neck, oval eyes, hypotonia (flaccid musculature), hypoplasia of the midphalanx of the fifth finger (a short middle bone in the little finger), a wide gap between the first and second toes, heart defects in 30 to 50 percent of cases, gastrointestinal defects in 10 percent of cases, and cervical instability due to poor development at C1 and C2.

Autism

Autism can be difficult to understand, but it helps to recall that "aut" comes from "auto," meaning "within oneself." The snowsports instructor of an autistic individual should be sensitive to the fact that the student's personality may be confined to a bubble. Often, the parent or care attendant is the only person who can regularly enter the bubble; look to this person for guidance on how to establish rapport with the student.

The causes of autism are unknown, but can be prenatal, viral, metabolic, or some form of epilepsy. It is a lifelong disability and can be severely incapacitating. It usually appears in the first three years of life and is more common in males by a ratio of 4 to 1. General symptoms include deficits in verbal or nonverbal communication and socialization and play, as well as repetitious body movements. Other symptoms include immature rhythms of speech, limited understanding of ideas, use of words without the usual meanings, and abnormal responses to sensations such as smells and sounds.

With IQ testing, 60 percent of autistic individuals are less than 50, 20 percent are between 50 and 70, and 20 percent are greater than 70. Some persons with autism—referred to as savants—have advanced skills in music, mathematics, and spatial conceptualization but are very limited in other ways. In severe cases, the student can be aggressive or self-injurious. No cure for autism is known at this time.

Instructors should be aware of other disorders that fall into the autism spectrum. These include **pervasive developmental disorder** (PDD), in which an individual exhibits deficits in social interaction but does not show other behaviors associated with autism, and **Asberger's syndrome**, in which the individual demonstrates deficits in social development, restricted range of interest, and behaviors associated with autism but has normal development of communication or cognitive skills.

Epilepsy

Epilepsy is the result of a temporary electrochemical imbalance within the regulatory mechanism of the brain. A sudden overload of energy may swamp the brain, causing partial or complete, brief or prolonged lapses in consciousness, known as epileptic seizures. It is estimated that one in every 100 hundred people may have some form of epilepsy. Four major types of seizure disorders are:

- **Grand mal**—This is the most dramatic type (literally, "big bad") and is characterized by a temporary loss of consciousness, rigidity, jerking of the extremities, and falling. An "aura" may warn the epileptic of an impending seizure, but not in time to warn others or get into a safe situation. Swallowing may be impaired, and bowel and bladder control may be affected, resulting in vomiting, urination, and/or defecation. The seizure may last from a few seconds to a few minutes.

  The appropriate action is to take the individual to a quiet area, place the person in a comfortable position, and protect from self-injury by supporting or padding the head. Contrary to popular belief, it is best to not place anything between the teeth. Upon awakening, the person will be embarrassed and exhausted. If this type of seizure occurs during a lesson, it is recommended to call the ski patrol for assistance. Some common medications to prevent grand mal seizures are Dilantin, phenobarbital, Tegretol, and Klonopin.

- **Petit mal**—This type ("little bad") normally appears as a blank stare during which mental processes cease, usually with no or only brief loss of consciousness. Other signs may include muscles that twitch and eyes that roll, blink rapidly, or remain fixed on a specific object.

  Following a petit mal seizure, assess the student's cognitive and physical state. Ask if the individual is experiencing nausea, dizziness, or double vision. Be aware that a series of petit mal seizures can lead to a grand mal seizure.

  Persons with petit mal seizures may or may not take medication.

- **Psychomotor and focal motor**—These seizures are less frequent and less severe. The individual may be confused, stagger, have twitching facial muscles, and make purposeless movements or unintelligible sounds. Following the seizure, recommend that the person rest.

Pharmacology 101

The information in this section is intended as a primer for the professional snowsports instructor who may be teaching or guiding adaptive skiers or snowboarders. For example, some antibiotics create a hypersensitivity to sun exposure. That overly sunburned woman you noticed in class may be having a such a reaction and is at risk of a serious burn as the day goes on. That teenager who had trouble understanding directions shortly after the hot chocolate break may be diabetic and is experiencing either a sugar overload or an insulin reaction in response to the sugar or exercise. Therefore, it is prudent to interview students regarding their disability and the medications they are taking. These students generally are aware of the potential side effects, but the instructor should become familiar with these as well.

Safety is the highest priority for snowsports instructors. Use of drugs, whether by prescription or for "recreational" purposes, may affect balance, communication, fatigue levels, and general performance. However, the use of appropriate drugs can prevent seizures, improve attention, and relieve depression.

Table 1.2 lists of some of the more commonly used drugs and their potential side effects. Note that Table 1.2 is only a partial list and remember that each of these medicines also has a generic name.

According to the National Association of Chain Drug Stores, the number of prescription drugs taken by Americans rises exponentially from year to year. Consumers fill 2.8 billion prescriptions per year, representing more than 11 prescriptions for every man, woman, and child in the United States. A typical senior citizen may use two to four different prescription drugs at the same time. Each year, more than 9 million adverse drug reactions occur in older Americans.

As an instructor or coach, be aware that any athlete seeking elite status may be subjected to drug testing. Even some of the more common cold medications may be considered "performance-enhancing" and may be considered illegal, leading to sanctions or banning from competitions. Contact the USADA (U.S. Anti-Doping Agency) at 1-800-233-0393 with any questions related to drugs, or check out their website at www.usantidoping.org.

TABLE 1.2 Commonly Used Drugs and Their Side Effects

Type	Example(s)	Uses	Side Effects
Antibiotic	Penicillin, Keflex, Ceclor, Cipro, Tetracycline	Infection	dizziness, drowsiness, sun sensitivity
Antispasm	Flexeril, Valium, Robaxin, Soma	Back pain, cerebral palsy	lethargy, blurred vision
Anti-inflammatory	Motrin, Advil, Naprosyn, Indocin	swelling, joint pain, arthritis, gout	headaches, rash, dizziness
Analgesic	Tylenol w/codeine, Percodan, Demorol	pain	sedation, rash, convulsions
Anti-Convulsant	Dilantin, Phenobarb, Klonopin, Tegretol	seizures	sun sensitivity, rash, blurred or double vision
Anti-Depressant	Elavil, Prozac, Zoloft	depression	drowsiness, dizziness, blurred vision
Anti-Coagulant	Coumadin, Heparin	blood clot prevention	hemorrhage
Anti-diabetic	Insulin, Diabinese, Glucophage	diabetes	nausea, vomiting, hypoglycemia

Student Assessment

chapter 2

The first and most critical part of every ski lesson is the student assessment or evaluation. To teach a successful lesson, the instructor must first have a complete picture of the student's particular goals and abilities to help create a realistic lesson plan. This is doubly important for adaptive skiers because of their more limited physical or cognitive capabilities, the need for specialized equipment suited to the specific situation, and the need for more highly customized lesson plans. The assessment must consider:

- Cognitive, affective, and physical aspects of the disability
- The student's stance and gait, balance, strength, and mobility
- Medications that the student is taking and associated side effects.

Components of the student assessment include a student information form, visual assessment, physical assessment, and cognitive assessment.

The **Student Information Form** is a questionnaire completed by the student, an aide, or family member before the first lesson. It provides general information on the student's disability and special medical considerations and has a section for tracking the student's progress. After each lesson, the instructor records the type of equipment and setup used and notes any information to help the next instructor pick up the lesson where it left off. Ideally, the student information form is available for the instructor's review prior to the lesson. (An example of a student information form is provided at the end of this chapter.)

The **Visual Assessment** begins as the student arrives for the lesson. It starts with general observations, becomes more specific, and then leads to inquiries about the skier's disability, medications, motivations, goals, and other activities. The following questions may help you, but use these only as a starting point and expand upon the questions as you see fit.

- Is the student in a wheelchair, using a walker or crutches, wearing leg braces or a prosthetic, walking with a cane? The student's mobility and need for special equipment give a good idea about the severity of the disability.
- Did the student need help opening the door? Turning a doorknob and pushing or pulling a door denotes a certain amount of grip strength and arm strength as well as a degree of independence.
- If the student is using a wheelchair, what type is it? The type of wheelchair and accessories can tell you about a student's balance and coordination and give insight into which muscle groups have paresis (partial paralysis or weakness).

- Is the student outgoing or withdrawn, excited or fearful, unreserved or having second thoughts? Knowing a student's attitude about the lesson can be a valuable aid in selecting the appropriate teaching style.
- Does the student look strong and athletic? A student who participates in sports and works out will probably learn fast. Be prepared to keep the lesson moving at an accelerated pace and to skip steps in the teaching progression if needed to maintain interest.
- Is the student dressed appropriately for the conditions? Lack of appropriate attire probably indicates a student who has never skied or ridden before. This student may be need special instruction about the winter environment or a slower lesson pace.

The **Physical Assessment** allows the instructor to gather specific information about the student's disability and physical condition beyond that provided in the student information form. Before conducting a physical assessment, ask questions that will help you understand your student's disability. The individual is an expert in the disability and can provide ample information. It is far better to ask questions up front than to put yourself in an uncomfortable situation later or, worse, endanger your student. The information gathered can guide you in selecting and teaching techniques:

- Does the student have any related or unrelated secondary disabilities? You must consider secondary disabilities when setting up equipment and teaching. For example, visual, hearing, or cognitive impairments may accompany multiple sclerosis, traumatic brain injury, or cerebral palsy.
- How long has the disability has been present? People with a recent injury may be weak or unaccustomed to their current situation.
- Has the student undergone major surgery within the last year? If so, the student may need a doctor's release or tire easily.
- Is the student taking any medications and, if so, what are the side effects? Keep a *Physician's Desk Reference* handy.

As you gather more information, the student may need to do some simple exercises to help you evaluate:

- **Functional Musculature**— determine which muscle groups the student can or cannot use.
- **Strength**—Evaluate the primary muscle groups needed for a specific discipline.
- **Balance**—Have the student lean to one side and return to upright, repeat to the other side, and then try it with eyes closed.
- **Coordination**—Watch the student perform physical tasks, with an eye for fluidity and efficiency of motion. (Watching the student

move around the room, open doors, or put on a jacket will help you assess gross motor movements. Watching the student write will give you an idea of the level of fine motor movements.)

- **Flexibility and Range of Motion**— Disabled students often have restricted range of movement due to joint fusion, muscle hypertonicity (rigidity), or muscle atrophy.
- **Motor and Sensory Deficits**— Use questions and simple tests to determine what parts of the body the student can feel and control. If the student has feeling in body parts with limited function, determine the types of sensations felt: heat, cold, pain, or pressure. If the student has incomplete sensation, determine the extent.
- **Vision and Hearing**—Some students may forget to mention secondary visual or auditory impairments that are less obvious than the primary impairment. In the case of a visual impairment, find out what the student can see. Vision should be tested both inside and outside to assess the effects of bright light and shadows. Find out if the student sees better out of one eye or the other. Impairment in one eye may cause a lack of depth perception. Test the student's field of vision as well as visual acuity. If the student has a hearing impairment, find out how severe it is. Does the student wear a hearing aid, read lips, or use sign language? Does the student hear better out of one ear than the other? All of these factors will influence how you conduct the lesson.

In addition to these physical issues, ask about the student's prior experience with skiing, snowboarding, and other sports. Did the student ski or

snowboard or participate in some other sport before becoming disabled? Prior athletes have good body awareness—an advantage when learning to ski or snowboard with adaptive equipment. If the student currently participates in another sport, you can usually draw similarities to help the student learn the snowsport.

The **Cognitive Assessment** occurs throughout the evaluation process. Evaluate the following to help you develop the best lesson plan for the particular student:

- Is the level of cognitive functioning appropriate for chronological age? Remember to address the student in a manner suitable to chronological age unless contraindicated by the assessment or other sources.
- Can the student hear, understand, and answer your questions?
- What is the person's emotional state: motivated, confident, timid, anxious, eager, elated, reserved, confused, or patient?
- Is the student easily distracted? Lack of concentration and reduced attention span are characteristic of some disabilities.
- Can the student easily process information, follow directions, and stay focused?
- What are the student's long-term goals and goals for the day? Motivation is key to developing the lesson plan for the day and for the future.

By the time a thorough student assessment has been completed, the instructor will have gained lots of important insights into the physical and cognitive abilities, special needs, and attitudes and personality traits of the student—insights needed to help tailor a specific approach in terms of equipment and teaching style.

STUDENT INFORMATION FORM

Name: _____

Phone: (___) _____

Address: _____

City: _____ State: ____ Zip: ____

Date of birth: _____

Sex: F M   Height: _____ Weight:* _____

* sit equipment limit 200 pounds

Describe your disability: _____
_____
_____

Current physician: _____

Physician's phone: _____

Medications (dosage, frequency, reason for use): _____
_____
_____
_____

Surgical procedures (include dates): _____
_____
_____
_____

General physical condition: Excellent Good Fair

Do you have seizures?   Yes   No

    Date of last seizure: _____

    Type: _____

Do you have a shunt?   Yes   No

Do you have allergies?   Yes   No

    Please list: _____
    _____

Do you have bladder or bowel adaptations? Yes No

    Type: _____

Mobility: walker crutches braces wheelchair
    Other: _____

Motor status: Please list any problems with **muscle tone, range of motion, or strength.** Also note any spasticity or paralysis and area affected.
_____
_____
_____

Please check any of the following that apply to you:

☐ Poor circulation in limbs
☐ Diabetes
☐ Cardiovascular problems
☐ Vision loss
☐ Hearing loss
☐ Sensory loss
☐ Respiratory problems
☐ Low endurance (tire easily)
☐ Communication difficulties
☐ Other: _____

BEHAVIOR & GENERAL ATTITUDES:

1 = normal
2 = mild problems, interferes infrequently
3 = moderate problems, interferes frequently
4 = severe problems, interferes constantly

Please enter above number to items below:
____ Frustration tolerance
____ Hostility
____ Confusion
____ Anxiety
____ Distractibility
____ Impulsivity
____ Following directions
____ Problem solving
____ Slowness of speech
____ Spatial disorientation
____ Memory loss (short-term)
____ Memory loss (long-term)
____ Temper
____ Ability to self correct
____ Aphasia (expressive)
____ Aphasia (receptive)

Please note any additional information that would assist us with your ski experience:
_____
_____
_____

What are your goals for your skiing experience?
_____
_____
_____

List names of other family members or friends who will be skiing with you:
_____
_____
_____

Developmental and Cognitive Disabilities

chapter 3

A **developmental disability** is one that is present at birth or arises during childhood. It can have a cognitive component, a physical component, or both. A **cognitive disability** is one that arises after age 18 and is related to learning impairment or attention deficit. Developmental and cognitive disabilities interrupt, delay, or reverse normal development. Quality adaptive lessons for students with these disabilities require that the instructor have at least a rudimentary knowledge of human development. See PSIA's *Core Concepts* manual for information on this topic.

When teaching individuals with a developmental or cognitive disability, the student assessment described in Chapter 2 will lead into a more specific appraisal of developmental/cognitive, social, emotional, behavioral, and learning characteristics to guide the instructor in developing a teaching plan.

As the lesson progresses, continued reassessment may suggest needed modifications. A key ingredient for success is to establish trust by listening actively, creating a friendly and mutually respectful atmosphere, and correctly interpreting behavior and personal style. As with the student assessment, this occurs throughout the lesson and requires patience, consideration, and care.

Because the vast majority of students with developmental/cognitive disabilities will be stand-up two-track skiers, basic exercises and suggestions in the *Alpine Technical Manual* provide a helpful and logical sequence for structuring lessons. Refer to Chapter 1 for disability descriptions and medical information. Much of the adaptation for developmental/cognitive disabilities involves presentation, while equipment adaptations and "hands-on" teaching methods expand the learning and teaching options available to the student and instructor.

Assessing Cognitive Development

Indications of arrested cognitive development include:

- **Seeing images but being unable to manipulate them mentally** (i.e., images cannot be transposed)—For example, if the instructor stands facing the student and demonstrates a wedge, the student will imitate the wedge with heels together and toes apart.

- **Acting impulsively and disregarding consequences**—A student may understand that an action will have undesirable consequences but cannot stop taking the action.

Questions to assist the instructor in assessing cognitive development include the following:

- What is the developmental age as well as the chronological age of the student? Begin by addressing the student according to chronological age. Later, communication styles can be adapted as the situation warrants. Sources of information for this assessment are the student, the caregiver, and any notes available from previous lessons.

- How does this student learn? Start by observing the student and asking some simple questions to assess the following:
  - ability to understand basic instructions or complex commands
  - short-term memory
  - attention span
  - ability to solve a simple problem
  - how easily distracted or confused
  - ability to verbalize thoughts
  - ability to imitate a simple movement patterns
  - receptivity to a "hands-on" approach

Becoming familiar with these qualities and the student's past experiences develops an atmosphere in which the student and the caregiver work with the instructor to develop a picture of how the student learns.

- Is the student motivated to ski or snowboard? Familial or societal support or interest in other sports can indicate motivation. Combat a lack of interest with a plan that capitalizes on an upbeat, positive presentation (e.g., using props to energize the student). A mutually realistic assessment of abilities and goals helps make the lesson a win-win situation for the student and instructor.

- Is the student's behavior appropriate? If the student cannot manage frustration or exhibits behavior inappropriate for a public setting (e.g., sexual gestures or use of profanities), consider behavior-modification techniques such as time-outs, modeling, motivators, written behavior contracts, deep breathing, and changes in environment. These techniques are addressed later in this chapter.

- What are the self-sufficiency and social skills of the student? Self-sufficiency skills include self-maintenance such as dressing, counting change, handling frustration, writing one's name, going to school, having a job, and living independently. Social skills include degrees of appropriate group behavior as well as one-on-one interaction. Common behaviors among those with brain injuries can include quietness or shyness (possibly accompanied by low self-esteem, depression, or lack of motivation) or impulsiveness, agitation, and aggression.

- What is the student's ability to communicate? Check to see if the student can articulate concerns and ideas. Note if speech is clear and check for correct language. Students with problems may be hampered in their ability to use words, have difficulty understanding what is meant, exhibit a delay in processing words, or be unable to react to a request. The student may become frustrated if told something repeatedly, "talked down to," or given a sequence of instructions that can be neither understood nor acted upon.

Assessing Physical Development

Just as cognitive development progresses in an orderly fashion through a person's early years, so too does physical development. While each person develops at a unique rate, the overall pattern is similar. For an in-depth discussion, refer to PSIA's *Children's Instruction Manual* (1997).

While physical development occurs through time, part of the progression is experiential. People the same age may have markedly different physical abilities due to different experiences. One person may have excellent eye-foot coordination because of playing soccer, while another has better eye-hand coordination from playing baseball. Each of these people can develop the other type of skill by taking the time to progress through the stages of movement development. Being aware of how people develop physically will help the instructor design progressions to move the students smoothly through the different stages.

Students with a cognitive and/or developmental disability often have neural (nervous system) impairment that affects brain/muscle connections and is expressed as non-normal movement patterns. The instructor must work within the abilities of the student to develop movement patterns that enable the student to ski.

Examples of questions that can help the instructor assess physical development are:

- What are the basic motor skills of the student? Watch closely as the student walks. Are the movements graceful or awkward, smooth or stiff? To assess balance, have the student stand on one leg and then the other. Notice body movements used for balance. Ask the student to move each limb separately and then in different combinations with each other to assess range of motion and coordination.

- Does the student have adequate strength? Test the student for muscle strength at each joint. Push against the direction of movement the student is attempting. For example, a standing student tries to push one leg to the side while the instructors resists that movement. Remember, ball-and-socket joints (hips, shoulders) have different ranges of motion than hinge joints (knees, elbows, wrists, fingers) or vertebral joints. Paralysis, paresis, and paresthesia (loss of feeling) may affect strength or movement of a limb. Last, inquire about the student's muscle tone and fatigue levels.

- Can the student bear weight on both feet when knees are flexed? In addition to absolute muscle strength, this is important in determining whether a student can successfully two-track ski and should be assessed before analysis for leg-length discrepancy, fore-aft motions, or pronation/supination. Note that in most but not all cases, these types of issues can be addressed by adjustments inside the boot.

What are the other manifestations of the student's disability? A student with a head injury may have impaired balance and coordination; a student with Down's syndrome may exhibit unusual looseness in the joints; a student with Parkinson's disease may sway to maintain balance. While generalizations may be made concerning physical manifestations of a specific disability, each person has individual abilities and limitations that a thorough assessment can determine.

Teaching Information

The teaching progression for developmental and cognitive disabilities closely follows the method set forth in PSIA's *Alpine Technical Manual*, which introduces a variety of innovative teaching approaches through its introduction of "zones" and the "stepping-stone" approach to parallel skiing. Please become familiar with this material.

In addition to using the information provided by the *Alpine Technical Manual*, the instructor needs to consider the student's comprehension level, sequencing abilities, and behavior to form a successful lesson plan. Instructors will also benefit from familiarity with the behavior modification techniques and teaching alternatives presented in this chapter.

USING FUN, GAMES, AND PROPS FOR LEARNING

Props can offer be very helpful in establishing physical boundaries for the student.

Examples include:

- tennis balls cut in half (to demarcate slalom courses)
- traffic cones (photo 3.1)
- edible treats (with permission)
- a Hula Hoop™ (photo 3.2)

- a Frisbee™
- a ball to toss
- colored dots for the gloves, boots, and skis (one color for the right, another for the left)
- food dye in squeeze bottles (combined with water to create "ribbons" in the snow)
- small slalom gates

- knee "eyeballs" (made by drawing or pasting paper eyes on a pair of kneepads)
- small flags on straws or wires
- a communication card—point to card for nonverbal communication (see fig. 3.1 on page 26)
- a teaching environment made up of props (e.g., a terrain garden)

PHOTO 3.1 Cones are suitable props for turning exercises.

PHOTO 3.2 A Hula Hoop™ provides contact and guidance.

FIGURE 3.1 Communication Card

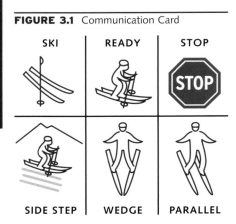

SKI	READY	STOP
SIDE STEP	WEDGE	PARALLEL

Source: *Ski Instruction for the Developmentally Disabled* (1990), used with permission

BEHAVIOR MODIFICATION

Behavior modification is the use of some system of reward or punishment to change undesirable behavior. The following examples may help when giving ski lessons:

- **Time-out**—A time-out is when the lesson is suspended for a prescribed amount of time. Avoid excess stimulation or any activity that may be regarded as pleasurable or rewarding. Use the time-out as a teaching aid, rather than punishment. A break in the action removes any positive reinforcement for the inappropriate behavior and gives the student a chance to change it. Remember the following time-out tips:
  - Make sure the length of the time-out fits the behavior.
  - Use the time-out to shift attention from the student's "manipulation" to your leadership and avoid overemphasizing the negative behavior.
  - Enforce the rules established at the start of the lesson consistently to avoid mixed messages.

- Respond to inappropriate behavior the first time rather than putting it off and hoping it is not repeated. Consider issuing a warning that allows the student to make the correct choice: *"You have a choice, Garrett. If you hit me again, we will go inside and stop skiing. If you don't hit me, we will keep skiing."*

- Be patient when using "discipline" and do not get angry; instead, be blasé. Students may have trouble distinguishing between positive and negative comments.

- The length of the time-out in minutes should equal the child's age.

Be firm when preventing or putting an end to inappropriate behavior. Try to use time-outs for the more aggressive or antisocial behaviors, such as hitting or talking back. For "minor" infractions, consider ignoring the behavior or redirecting it to another activity. Forget about softening the blow of a time-out. Simply tell the student when the time-out is over, and then act as if nothing unusual has happened.

- **Modeling behavior**—Through modeling, the instructor can guide the student toward appropriate and effective interactions on the hill. Students will tend to imitate the instructor at even the subtlest level. They duplicate not only behavior, but also attitudes; keep yours positive. Also, be aware of the potential to change a student's behavior by positive reinforcement of the good examples set by other students in the lesson.

- **Motivators**—These can range from favorite munchies (dispensed with discretion, since the person could have a developmental disability that includes a food obsession) to using a number system to count down the remaining runs until going in for a treat. Returning to a student's favorite run or lending the student a favorite article of clothing (e.g., a colorful scarf, hat, or mittens) might also be used as motivators. Experiment with methods that stimulate the student and provide an incentive to continue.

- **Written behavior contracts**—If the student has a history of behavior problems, a simple, one-line contract such as "I promise to ski safely and keep my speed down on the hill" may suffice. The student and instructor sign the contract, and the instructor then keeps it handy during the lesson and shows it to the student as needed. Be sure that the student has the intellectual capacity to understand the concept of a contract.

- **Deep breathing**—This can be used as a relaxation technique. Have the student stop and take a deep breath or do rhythmic breathing exercises to relax the mind and muscles.

- **Environmental changes**—Removing the student from an over-stimulating or threatening environment can bring about behavior change or calmness. Examples of negative environmental stimuli are noisy, crowded buildings, loud snowmaking guns, or the presence of an overprotective caregiver. Simply move the student to another location.

Teaching Information
BEGINNER/NOVICE ZONE

Much can be accomplished indoors if time and patience permit. An indoor setting allows the instructor to introduce new skills without the distraction of an unfamiliar and slippery environment. Among the elements of a quality lesson that can be taught indoors are

- familiarity with equipment
- fundamentals of a skiing stance
- boot drills
- warm-ups
- stretching exercises

In addition to helping develop rudimentary skills, indoor activities allow time for bonding with the student. After instructor and students have donned their boots, any or all of the following indoor exercises may be introduced:

- Walk throughout the facility.
- Climb stairs to simulate side-stepping.
- Maneuver through an obstacle course made with common objects. For example, use flags, chairs or benches, cones, tape, and/or brightly colored objects. Set up "stations" that include turns and walking high, then low.
- Try "Pop Goes the Weasel" with feet on or off the ground. Everyone crouches while singing "pop goes the weasel" and then stands or jumps up at the word "pop."
- Put on skis and move around on a carpeted floor. The padding provided by the carpeting reduces the fear of hard falls.
- Place masking tape on the floor in wedge, parallel, side-step, and circle patterns. By placing their feet, and perhaps later their skis, on the patterns, the students can get a feel for the movements they will be performing on snow.

- Show ski films and pictures of skiing to help motivate the students.

When the student becomes comfortable with indoor activities and the instructor, it is time to move outside. Find a flat or nearly flat area and try some of the following exercises:

- Do simple exercises that do not require ski poles.
- Walk alongside the student, with the student inside a Hula Hoop™, or outside of the hoop while holding onto it.
- Set up a slalom course for the student to walk/shuffle/slide through.
- Recheck the boots and, if necessary, unbuckle the top buckle to allow a greater range of ankle flexion.
- Perform high-low exercises, with hands on hips or knees.
- Tell the student to "le-e-a-a-n forward, l-e-e-a-a-n back," while stationary.
- This is a good time to teach how to get up off the snow. Effective techniques are the roundup and V-up. For the **roundup**, the student lies on the uphill hip and places the skis across the fall line with the hands uphill just forward of the feet. The student straightens the legs while pushing the buttocks into the air and "walking" the hands downhill, then pushes to a standing position. For the **V-up**, the student lines up with the fall line, positions the feet in an inverted wedge, and pushes off the snow (hips first).
- If possible, teach the herringbone and show how to uncross skis.

Sliding and Gliding, Straight Run

- Glide on gentle terrain with a terrain-assisted stop.
- Encourage a tall, upright stance with eyes forward. Cue the student by saying, "Look forward at me," and "Hold a tray with your hands." Use familiar images.
- Work on dynamic balance (balance in motion) by reaching forward, leaning back, and then staying in the middle.
- Ski or walk next to the student, providing support with a ski pole or a bamboo pole. Or, ski backwards, offering verbal cues and helping the student focus on the task.
- Use a ski bra (photo 3.3 on page 28) and spacer bar if additional assistance is needed.
- For students who also have a physical impairment, consider using a walker or outriggers for support.

Deciding Whether to Teach the Wedge or Direct-to-Parallel

The following is a traditional wedge-to-parallel progression. Various choices of skill development progressions are now available with the introduction of short, shaped skis. The *Alpine Technical Manual* outlines many "stepping stone" paths to parallel skiing. Refer to pages 35 to 51 of the *Alpine Technical Manual* for additional information and options.

Introducing the Wedge

- Introduce the wedge by having the student move the legs apart and turn the toes inward.
- Develop the first wedge movements on flat terrain. Use flexion and extension to help develop the movements.

- If needed, ski bras, spacer bars, and bamboo poles can be great tools at this stage to assist in creating a balanced stance. These are teaching tools and not a permanent piece of equipment.
- Encourage ankle and knee flexion by helping the student actively work the boot while in motion. Perform "Wilt and Mickeys" (i.e., high and low stances *a la* Wilt Chamberlain and Mickey Mouse). To keep the hips centered, "squash bugs" under both feet.
- If the student sits back against the boot, the instructor should ski backwards in front, with the student's hands on top. This may also be performed using a horizontal pole held between the student and instructor. Those actions reposition the student's stance.

First Turns
- While gliding in the wedge, the student looks in the desired direction of travel and turns the toes, feet, and legs in the same direction.
- If needed, use physical assists such as tip holds (in which the instructor skis backward, holding the student's ski tips) and two-point holds (i.e., instructor's skis are placed between the student's skis, while instructor places one hand on the student's hip and one hand on the student's outside knee) to generate the feeling of steering.
- Use additional props to assist in the development of steering movements. The student can hold a round object such as a Hula Hoop™ or bicycle tire in front like a steering wheel, turning the wheel and the feet at the same time. The instructor can use an object suspended from a pole (like a carrot on a stick) to encourage the student to look in the direction of intended travel.

PHOTO 3.3 Using a Ski Bra

Deacon Chapin Photography

- Turn around objects on the snow, such as cones and halved tennis balls.

If the student does not know left from right, the instructor can ski backwards in front of the student. Props such as tape on one mitten can be used to cue the direction of the turn: ("toward the tape, away from the tape").

The student might lean uphill away from the turn, which negates the effect of rotary and pressuring movements of the legs and feet. Use props, games, or exercises to get the skier to move in the direction of the turn (e.g., have the skier slide the outside hand down the outside of the leg from the hip toward the knee).

Fatigue and lack of balance or muscle tone might cause the student to tip downhill while attempting the first turn. Keep introducing games, props, and exercises to help achieve a proper stance. If continued efforts prove unsuccessful, physical assists (photo 3.4) or equipment (outriggers, a walker, reins, ski bras, and spacer bars) may help.

Riding the Chairlift
Before venturing onto lift-served terrain, be sure that the student can ski the slopes serviced, then teach the student to safely load, ride, and unload the lift. Because chairlift safety is crucial to a quality lesson, spend time preparing the student. For example, you can practice loading and unloading before getting into the lift line using a bench. Or, you can show a video or provide an opportunity for the student to observe other skiers loading the lift while you explain what is happening.

Have a plan for how to get on and off the chairlift with the student. It is helpful to communicate with lift operators in advance so they are familiar with student's needs and the optimal chairlift speed for both loading and unloading. Having the student speak with the operator can help personalize the process. Place special emphasis on securing seizure-prone students. Some ski areas require use of a climbing harness with a triple-stitched retention

PHOTO 3.4 A skier assist can help generate the feeling of steering.

Deacon Chapin Photography

strap that attaches around a chairlift rung. Check the student's equipment to see if it is properly attached. If extra help is required to carry adaptive equipment or push the student into place, try to line up a volunteer in advance. If you have any doubt about the student's understanding of the unloading process, calmly recap the correct procedure while on the chairlift. Try to instill confidence so that the student does not become frightened.

Linking Turns
- The student follows as you link turns on beginner terrain.
- Set up small cones, pine cones, or other soft objects for the student to turn around.
- Use food coloring or colored water to draw a line for the student to follow.
- If needed, have the student hold a pole horizontally out in front. The instructor may hold this pole while skiing backwards to lead the student through the turns.

- Use a ski bra and reins if additional assistance is needed. The instructor controls speed and can "pull" a turn from behind. If available, a volunteer can ski backwards in front of the student, performing "follow-me" turns.

On gentle terrain, your student should be able to begin linking turns with little instruction. For whatever reason—fear, lack of fear, lack of skill, or the thrill of going straight downhill—your student may not want to make a turn! This obviously will cause problems for you and potentially cause problems for the student and other guests on the mountain. The challenge is to find a way to motivate the student to turn. Make up a game such as "parallel park contest" (the student turns around a prop and "parks" next to it). Or, offer a reward for something the student might want to do ("If we make 10 turns, we can go up the chairlift again").

Moving Toward Parallel Turns
- Increase speed on familiar and comfortable terrain.
- Turn or steer the inside leg to match the outside leg.
- Change the edge of the inside ski.
- Tap the uphill ski lightly on the snow.

If the student does not understand the difference between wedge and parallel turns, show pictures (see fig. 3.1 on page 26), practice on flatter terrain, and break the positions into smaller components. Use simple commands: "Wedge, parallel, make a "V" with the skis, make an 11 with the skis."

When students are reluctant to leave the comfort of the wedge, continue progress toward independent leg action by allowing them to make wide, almost bowlegged parallel turns, as long as the ski comes to a neutral standing position at the finish of the turn.

Getting the skis parallel early in the turn can be scary for some students. You may need to revert to physical assists such as a two-point hold, tip hold, or horse-and-buggy assist with bamboo poles to help the student steer the inside ski. (A horse-and-buggy assist is a method for guiding either from in front or behind the skier, with both instructor and skier holding a guiding object, such as a bamboo pole.)

INTERMEDIATE ZONE
Introducing Pole Use
- Practice the pole swing and touch, without skis on, on flat terrain.
- Encourage extend-touch and flex-retract movements while practicing on the flats.
- Play "follow-the-leader" by having the student copy your pole timing and use.
- Use a specific rhythm to time pole use (tall, touch, turn).

Pole use can be difficult for some students. Break down the task, introducing one component at a time. Start with static exercises and then progress to a single turn in one direction. Work on the timing of the single turn before linking turns. Use visual cues such as colored spots on the snow or very small moguls to help with starting the pole swing and with timing. Call out commands for timing the pole touch.

Exercises for Parallel Turns

- Stand on flat terrain in ski boots, swiveling both feet together to turn side to side. Repeat with skis on. Next, move to a gentle slope and have the student twist both skis into the fall line. The turn is completed with the familiar skidding movement, and the student then uses extension movements to ease into the next turn.
- Use a parallel christie (i.e., skidding skis on corresponding edges) progression, moving from a complete traverse to heading downhill to crossing the fall line in a parallel turn.

- Try hop turns. Have the student make turns using three small hops, then two, then one, and scale this back to an extension movement to initiate a turn.
- Ski patience turns. From a tall stance, the student lets the tips drift into the fall line. Gravity helps initiate the turn. Encourage flexing down and inward and steering the legs and feet to complete the turn.

If the student does not have the attention span or understanding for explanations of skill development and step-by-step progressions, keep it simple and fun. Do the movements instead of describing them. Add rhythm and change the speed and shape of the wedge christie to produce an often "magic" transition to parallel turns.

Some students continue to have problems controlling speed. Emphasize steering the skis across the fall line to complete each turn. You may want the student to try turning to a stop in each direction. Shorten the stops until the turns are controlled and linked.

Safety Note: As students progress, they will eventually spend time skiing without an instructor. They often attempt more difficult terrain, even if they are not ready. Make sure students understand and follow **Your Responsibility Code.** *Teach them how to read trail maps and determine which trails are appropriate. Any student unable to read trail maps, understand safety rules, or follow the responsibility code should be accompanied by a buddy or instructor.*

ADVANCED ZONE
In the advanced zone, the instructor continues to use teaching techniques and communication patterns appropriate for students with developmental or cognitive disabilities, although at higher speeds and on more challenging terrain and more varied snow conditions. Make sure that your student is prepared to experience all the mountain has to offer by progressively introducing more conditions and activities.

Refer to the *Alpine Technical Manual* for additional ideas, exercises, and suggestions for skiers at this level. Most important, have fun!

Blindness and Low Vision

chapter 4

Although this chapter focuses on adaptations needed to teach blind or visually impaired skiers, much of the information also applies for blind or visually impaired snowboarders. The information presented is not a substitute for experience, which is the primary avenue for learning how to teach these students. Although no two students or lessons are alike, the following outline is generally applicable.

It may be difficult for people with "normal" vision to relate to low vision or blindness, particularly the loss of equilibrium, feeling of dependence on the guide or instructor, and reliance on other senses. It therefore is surprising that teaching people with blindness or low vision is probably the easiest technique to adapt to an alpine progression.

Most of these skiers still follow the basic progression described in the *Alpine Technical Manual*. The primary adaptation is how to present the lesson, usually in an auditory or kinesthetic way, to optimize learning. In some cases, the student may have enough vision to allow you use a more visual approach. In other cases, the student may have low vision combined with another disability that requires you to combine

approaches. This is often the case for students who have a brain injury or a disease such as cancer, diabetes, or multiple sclerosis (MS). Congenital blindness can also be accompanied by cerebral palsy or other complications.

How the Eye Works

The eye works in much the same way as a camera. The front parts of the eye (cornea, pupil, and lens) are clear and allow light to pass through. Light also passes through the eyeball. Known as the vitreous cavity, this area is filled with a clear, jelly-like substance called vitreous humor or vitreous gel, which helps maintain the globose shape of the eyeball. The light is then focused on a thin layer of tissue called the retina, which covers the inside wall at the back of the eye. The retina is like the film in a camera—light hitting it forms a picture that transmitted to the brain through the optic nerve. This is how we see.

The retina has two parts: the macula and the peripheral retina. If you imagine the retina as a circular target, the macula is like the small bull's eye, while the surrounding area is the peripheral retina. The peripheral retina allows peripheral vision, i.e., vision to the side. However, because the peripheral retina is not able to see detail clearly, we cannot use

peripheral vision to read, thread a needle, drive, or even recognize a face. If you see someone off to your side, "out of the corner of your eye," you may be able to tell who it is because you recognize the person's general shape, but you will be unable to see facial expression, for example. To see fine detail, you must look straight ahead so that light from the image strikes the macula, which is approximately 100 times more sensitive to detail.

Students with blindness or low vision may be taking some of the following drugs for their condition. See Chapter 1 for a description of the effects and potential side effects of these medications:

- Antibacterials
- Anticonvulsants
- Antiemetics
- Beta-blockers
- Calcium channel blockers
- Carbonic anhydrase inhibitors
- Cardiac glycosides
- Diuretics
- Pilocarpine

Assessing the Extent of the Disability

Prior to selecting equipment or developing a lesson plan, evaluate the nature and extent of the disability by assessing the following—in addition to the overall student assessment described in Chapter 2:

- Does the student have any useable vision? This can be determined initially by observing the skier. Notice whether the student wears glasses, walks self-guided with a cane or with the assistance of a guide or guide dog, or moves about independent of these aids.
- Does the student have useable vision, is it in one or both eyes, and how does it differ between eyes? This information will help you determine how to guide your skier both on and off the hill.
- Can the student distinguish colors and shapes? Which colors are the easiest to identify in bright sunlight and shadows? Someone who cannot distinguish colors will have to "learn the mountain" and not rely on color-coded trail markers for terrain decisions based on degree of difficulty.
- How near or far can the student see? What is the acuity, depth perception, and angle of vision? Is the student's vision better inside or outside? Photo 4.1 shows assessment indoors and outside.

You can answer these questions in a variety of ways. Ask your student questions or use a simple assessment technique such as holding up a certain number of fingers at varying distances and angles. Assess one eye at a time, then both eyes. Use the results of your assessment and information from the student to show you how best to teach and guide this particular individual. For example, students with some vision may be able to follow as you ski, but only within a certain distance.

Equipment Selection and Set-up

A variety of equipment is available to help you teach students who are blind or have low vision. These include:

- Ski bra
- Bamboo poles
- Reins
- Blind athlete/guide bibs
- Personal two-way radios

See Chapter 6 for a description of these aids.

Safety Note: When teaching or guiding someone who is blind or visually impaired, keep in verbal or physical contact at all times; wear bibs to identify yourselves to other skiers or riders on the mountain; and keep some distance from the edge of the trail. Be mindful of any circulatory problem your student may experience. Routinely check hands and feet for warmth and beware of medication side effects. Have your student wear sunglasses or goggles to protect the eyes from wind and sun.

Communication Techniques

Personal two-way radios have become popular over the last few years and help instructors by eliminating the need to yell. Radios come with voice activation and hands-off microphones that fit conveniently into a helmet. The radio batteries should be checked regularly and an alternate signaling system established in

PHOTO 4.1 Assess vision outdoors as well as indoors.

Deacon Chapin Photography

case of signal failure. For the safety of your student, yourself, and others on the slopes, establish emergency commands. Instruct your student to "slow down," "sit down" (to the side), or "stop" immediately when you call out the emergency command. The commands are used when an out-of-control skier or snowboarder is rapidly approaching, if your student takes a wrong turn, or if you fall.

Voice inflection is important. Use a firm, confident tone to establish a trusting bond, but remember that not everyone with a disability is hard of hearing.

Directional commands are used to move the student from point to point. Different techniques include the clock system, verbal commands, auditory cues, and the grid system.

- **Clock system**—Relates to the numbers on a clock face and is most often used in a static situation. Twelve o'clock is always the direction your student is facing, with three o'clock and nine o'clock at 90° angles to the right and left, respectively. This system is also convenient when maneuvering through the lift line.
- **Grid system**—A good way for some students to visualize the slope and where they will be on that run. For example, you can describe the run as: "10 zones wide, with a total width of 50 yards; we'll stay in zones 2 to 6." This helps the student understand the position on the slope and the size of turn to make. The grid and clock systems should not be used together.
- **Auditory cues**—Consists of the instructor tapping ski poles together or clapping while skiing backward and facing the student. The student can tell from the

direction of the sound which way to turn. This approach also allows constant auditory connection with the instructor, which is comforting for most blind or visually impaired students as they are still gaining confidence, while saving the instructor's voice.

- **Verbal commands**—The most frequently used directional commands. The "hands-off" aspect of these cues enable the student to establish a rhythm and develop confidence by focusing on their movement. Familiarize the student with the commands before starting to ski: for example, "right turn, left turn" or "and turn, and turn." "Hold, hold, hold" can be used after a turn to indicate that the skier should traverse. The cadence of the commands is very important—at the correct speed and with predictable spacing to allow rhythm and flow.

Describe approaching terrain with words such as "dip," "flats," "steeps," "washboard," "rut," "bumps," or "small mounds" rather than "moguls," "smooth," or "groomed." Avoid a constant stream of nonessential chatter, which can tire the instructor and cognitively overload the student.

Guiding Techniques

Once you and your student have established commands and emergency procedures, you must agree upon communication strategies and guiding positions. The student may have a preference to which you, as the guide, should be able to adapt. A new skier or snowboarder may not have a preference. In this case, explain options and suggest what might work best.

Guiding a blind skier or snowboarder is one of the most challenging aspects of being an adaptive instructor. It is an ongoing process, through which the student and instructor, or participant and guide, learn each other's capabilities and desires. You have the ability to directly influence what the student can accomplish. It is both a team effort and a great challenge in the world of snowsports instruction.

GUIDING INSIDE THE LODGE, CORRALS, AND ON THE FLATS

- **Inside the lodge**—When walking with a blind person, let the student stand next to you and hold onto your elbow while staying about a half step behind. Move your elbow forward, and the student walks forward; move your elbow to the right, and the student moves to the right; and so forth. These non-auditory directional commands also apply to a pole lead or pole guiding (grip end held by the student, basket held by the instructor), used in long catwalks or flat transitional terrain.
- **Corrals and lift lines**—The student places one hand on your shoulder, and you glide through the maze of skiers as a unit. A pole lead can also be used. Small directional changes can be initiated using the elbow technique.
- **Catwalks and transitional terrain**—Use a pole lead to guide the student. Applying minimal pressure to the right or left (coupled with some verbal directions) will assist the student in moving in the desired direction.

GUIDING FROM THE FRONT WHILE SKIING OR SNOWBOARDING BACKWARDS

Skiing or snowboarding backwards (as shown in photo 4.2) is commonly used with first-time students because being downhill from them is very reassuring. Probably most important, it allows the instructor to control the student's speed and direction for a safer, more successful learning environment. Always be aware of the surroundings when sliding backwards.

GUIDING FROM THE SIDE

This is used for students who have peripheral vision (see photo 4.3). It can be difficult on a crowded slope, because as the student turns away from you, you must look uphill to check for safety. This requires that you momentarily take your eyes off the student.

GUIDING FROM BEHIND

This technique allows the student to easily hear your voice and enables you to easily observe skiing technique, give further instructions, and maintain a view of the slope and obstacles ahead (see photo 4.4).

The "Horse and Buggy" technique (photo 4.5) using bamboo poles may also be used for the blind skier or snowboarder who has demonstrated skiing fundamentals such as balance and the ability to form a wedge and turn but who needs a more hands-on approach. You can reinforce verbal instructions by giving the pole a half twist on the side of the intended turn.

PHOTO 4.2 Guiding from the Front, Skiing Backwards

Deacon Chapin Photography

PHOTO 4.3 Guiding from the Side

Deacon Chapin Photography

GUIDING FROM THE FRONT WHILE SKIING OR SNOWBOARDING FORWARD

This is commonly used for advanced skiers and snowboarders, particularly on a race course, but requires that you turn your head back over your shoulder to project your voice. Because this level of student is inevitably moving faster than a novice student, the technique requires expert skills from the instructor as well as development of a close instructor-student relationship built on trust and considerable time together (photo 4.6).

PHOTO 4.4 Guiding from Behind

Brian W. Robb

PHOTO 4.5 The horse and buggy may use the guide either in front or behind the skier.

Deacon Chapin Photography

PHOTO 4.6 A racer following close behind his guide.

Brian W. Robb

Teaching Information

The following exercises provide a variety of ideas for teaching a skier or snowboarder with blindness or low vision, from beginner/novice through advanced zones. Most lessons for these participants are on a one-to-one basis to ensure the student's safety and maximize the potential for success by modifying the lesson plan to match the student's individual abilities and needs.

The most important element of a lesson for a person with blindness or low vision is the expertise of the guide, and the best way to learn how to guide is to practice with another sighted person in a practical setting. The ski and snowboard progressions for people with blindness or low vision closely follow the progressions set forth by PSIA in the *Alpine Technical Manual* and other discipline-specific technical manuals, including the *Level I, Level II, and Level III Study Guides* (PSIA 1996).

BEGINNER/NOVICE ZONE

Because even partially sighted students may have difficulty seeing your demonstrations, a hands-on approach can be especially effective for blind or visually impaired participants. Make sure that students are comfortable with this type of teaching style by asking for permission before touching them—for example, by moving their hands or head into a more appropriate position. Avoid startling a student with an unexpected touch.

Introduce the Equipment

It is crucial that you acquaint these students with their equipment before they don it. Becoming familiar with the size, shape, and purpose of their gear will allow the students to relate more fully to the experience.

Help with the boots. Show the student how to put the boots on efficiently and adjust the buckle system. Emphasize that the boot should be snug but comfortable. Make sure the student knows how the binding works and learns options for releasing the binding. Before handing skis to a student, explain that they have sharp edges.

Let the student feel the equipment carefully (photo 4.7 on page 36) and practice donning it—including stepping into and releasing bindings in a stationary setting. A student can learn to step into the bindings by placing the sole of the ski boot on top of the toe binding and slowly drawing the foot directly backwards until the toe of the boot slips off the toe binding and into place. Pressure may then be placed on the heel to lock the heel binding. A ski pole held in each hand and planted in the snow can offer balance during this activity.

Show the basics of the poles. Describe them as having a basket and a handle and that the end is pointed. Teach the student how to carry the skis and poles. He or she needs to know how to properly carry ski equipment to avoid hitting objects or other people. Without an introduction to equipment, your student could develop faulty and possibly intimidating perceptions of what is in store.

After the student is familiar with the equipment, show the person how to get into a balanced, athletic stance and how to use the equipment correctly.

Use your enthusiasm about the sport and a positive description of the equipment to build excitement for the sport.

Flatland Drills and Exercises

- Students learn mostly by feeling or doing. Some analogies may be appropriate to help make a point. Describing motion by using word pictures incorporating familiar movements or objects can help make a point.
- A word picture of the environment may also help. It should include a description of the terrain and general surroundings such as snow makers, the presence of other guests, the chairlift maze, and so forth.
- Stress good hand position as you teach how to move in a balanced position.
- Emphasize how the shin should feel on the tongue of the boot and encourage ankle flex to help "stay forward."
- Stress a tall stance, comparing good hand position to carrying a lunch tray. Tell the student to point the thumbs forward—this results in the pole baskets being positioned just behind the boot.
- Ask what sensations the person feels from the feet, legs, the snow, and the environment.
- Check for understanding of tasks, pace of lesson, and endurance.

Sliding and Gliding, Straight Run Exercise

- Guide the student on a straight run on shallow terrain with a natural stop. Encourage a slightly flexed stance, with eyes and hands forward. Spend time helping the student identify foot sensitivity in the boot.

PHOTO 4.7 Touch the Equipment

Deacon Chapin Photography

BLIND SKIER

- Develop ankle and knee flex by asking the student to move smoothly up and down. Work on eliminating static positions. Have the student move forward by pressuring the tongue of the boot or moving the hands and hips forward.
- Comfort the tentative student by skiing or walking alongside while holding the persons closest pole just below the handle.
- Ski backwards in front, offering appropriate verbal cues to enhance body position and assure them that they are safe. Provide positive feedback often.

Skiers with low or no vision often have trouble differentiating a slow speed from being stationary. To help in this regard, the student can gently drag the tips of the poles next to the heels to provide tactile feedback. Be sure to encourage proper hand and body position if allowing the poles to drag on the snow.

Encourage the student to keep both skis flat with equal weight on each foot. After asking a student's permission, place the hands and feet in the correct position.

Stress the importance of keeping the chin level and the face pointed straight ahead. This serves several functions: it is the best position for following verbal and visual guiding; helps with stance and balance; and helps absorb uneven terrain.

Introduce the Wedge, Gliding, and Braking

- Introduce the wedge by having the student move the legs apart and turn the toes inward.
- Develop the first wedge movements on flat terrain. Use flexion and extension to help develop the movements.
- Assign numbers, names, or sizes to the various sizes of a wedge to distinguish between a gliding wedge and a braking wedge (e.g., one, two, three, or tiny, small, large).
- Comfort a tentative student by skiing or walking alongside while holding the person's closest pole just below the handle.

- Ski backwards in front, offering verbal cues to enhance body position and assure the student that he or she is safe. Provide positive feedback.

If the student continues to have difficulty differentiating a slow speed from being stationary, try skiing backwards with the person's outstretched palms against yours to maintain a balanced, athletic stance as you both come to a stop.

First Turns

- Using your student's hands to represent the skis, explain how the skis will be positioned throughout the turn (photo 4.8).
- Make sure the student maintains a good wedge position after the turn. Initially, try a verbal "follow me" approach. If this is unsuccessful, use an alternative approach such as verbal commands, horse and buggy, or reins.

PHOTO 4.8 Using the Hands to Explain Ski Position

Deacon Chapin Photography

- You may want to use a technique such as a tip hold or two-point hold to give the student a chance to feel a turn. At this point, you are trying to help the student achieve a steered turn. Make sure the student has a good stance on flat skis and is looking in the direction of the turn.

Riding the Chairlift

Help students learn how to ride the chairlift safely and with minimal physical and verbal cueing. Since ski area policies differ, check your area's guidelines before the lesson.

Explain the type of chairlift you are about to ride (e.g., double, triple, quad, center pole). It is helpful to practice loading before getting into the lift line. This can be done using a chair, either indoors or outdoors. Practicing a countdown (e.g., "three, two, one, sit") can help the student develop a feeling for what to expect. Establishing commands for maneuvering through the lift line is also helpful. Examples include "tips left," "tips right," "straight forward," "slide," or "shuffle." Students may be able to guide themselves through lift lines if they are positioned next to ropes or bars that delineate the corral or queue. The ropes or bars may be lightly touched with the shaft of a pole or the fingertips but should not be pulled against.

During the chair-loading sequence, the student can either take your arm or rely solely on verbal cues. When you and the student are side-by-side on the "wait here" board, the operator will cue you to move forward. For less experienced or less mobile students, or those with more complex equipment, it normally works better to position them between the lift operator and the instructor when loading. Upon reaching the "load here" board, students should crouch slightly and

reach behind the hips with one free hand to meet the chair, while continuing to face forward to keep from bumping their head on the lift support bar (bale). Returning to the verbal countdown you used during practice will help the student feel comfortable. Remind the student to not try and retrieve an item that is dropped while loading (e.g., a pole or glove) but to leave it for the operator to send up.

On the first chairlift ride, or whenever you feel that the student is not quite ready for normal loading, ask the operator to slow the lift. Check for loose clothing or equipment and remind the student that this is an important part of loading.

On the ride up, review instructions for getting off the lift, which are similar to those for a sighted skier. Because the student cannot see the unloading area, describe the pitch of the ramp and which way to turn after skiing down it. Instruct the student to stay down in the event of a fall during unloading to prevent being struck by the chair. As you approach the dismounting point, remind the student to keep the tips up and then count down to the touchdown: "Three, two, one, stand up." Something simple such as "nose over toes" can promote a balanced stance and successful dismount.

Have the student push off the from the chair with one hand, while holding onto you or the poles with the other and skiing straight off until you give a command to turn or stop. If the student is apprehensive or needs extra help, grasp the hand closest to you and tuck that arm between your arm and body. Use a firm forward motion of your arm and upper body to rise out of the chair. The arm of a taller student may need to rest atop the instructor's arm.

Linking Turns

- The cadence of your commands is crucial for students to develop linked, rhythmic turns.
- Make your students aware that they can control speed and direction through the size of the wedge and turn shape. Promote active steering of the inside leg to complement the action of the outside leg.
- Help your students refine guiding techniques by exploring wedge size and turn shape.
- Introduce flexion and extension by describing the range of movement. While students are static, verbally guide them through the range of movement discussed. Create guiding commands to incorporate flexion and extension, such as "extend and flex," using the cadence of your words to indicate the pace at which these actions should happen. Remember to show the students that flexion and extension movements should occur in a lateral/forward plane rather than straight up and down. Keep it simple and consistent.
- Encourage students to keep the inside leg flexed, guiding the ski in the same direction as the outside ski, while keeping the body centered between the skis. Review foot/leg steering versus trying to turn with the upper body. Practice boot arc exercises in the snow without skis.

Students may exhibit excessive head movements while struggling to concentrate on the new task of linking turns and listening carefully to you at the same time. Limit your commands to the essential and position yourself so that the student can focus on your voice without compromising good ski position.

Moving Toward Parallel Turns

- On comfortable terrain, encourage spontaneous matching of skis through increased speed, steeper pitch, and tighter turn radius.
- Adapt standard exercises to your student's needs such as thousand steps, garlands, thumpers, and fan progressions (see glossary for these exercises). More exercises may be found in the *Alpine Handbook* (PSIA 1996).
- Introduce an earlier matching of the skis—i.e., before the fall line. Help the student control speed control through turn shape and increased edging skills.
- Discuss turns in terms of cadence and circumference: "short," "medium," and "long." A slalom turn is short, a giant slalom turn is medium, and a super-G turn is long. The intonation of your voice assists in developing rhythm. For short, quick turns, you might say, "Turn and turn and turn and turn," whereas for medium turns you might opt for, "Turrrn annnd turrrn annnd turrrn annnd turrrn," etc.
- A wedge position creates a wide, stable foundation, so students are often reluctant to move into the less stable parallel position. Students must be ready to venture out of that comfort zone and use independent leg action as the process begins. Do exercises that emphasize independent leg action, such as skating or thousand-steps drills. Student need to be comfortable with slightly higher speeds and consistently skiing in small, gliding wedges. Often, you know that a student is expanding the comfort zone when ski matching happens spontaneously and speeds are being controlled.

- Emphasize the feeling of a flat ski. The student may need to roll the knees uphill to achieve flat skis. Practice a static exercise to work on developing a student's awareness of when skis are flat or edged and how to change the position with ankle and knee movements.

INTERMEDIATE ZONE
Introducing Pole Use

- Discuss pole use before introducing the pole swing and tap.
- With students in a parallel stance, encourage using both poles to push across the flats.
- Practice a stationary pole swing, focusing on lateral/forward ankle and knee extension in the direction of the new turn and wrist action to place the pole properly.
- Emphasize rhythm through counting or singing.
- Between turns in a traverse, begin touching the downhill pole lightly. This helps focus forward and downhill. Always accompany a pole touch with ankle and knee extension in the direction of the new turn.
- Make wedge christie turns in the fall line, using pole swing to coordinate flow between turns.
- Use pole swing and tap exercises and commands to help establish rhythm.
- To the tune of "Happy Birthday," sing the appropriate commands: "Plant your left pole, turn left; plant your right pole, turn right; plant your left pole, turn left; plant your right pole, turn right" (and many more!).
- While in a traverse, the student taps three times with the downhill pole prior to turning, i.e., "tap, tap, tap, turn." Remove a tap: "tap, tap, turn." After removing another tap, they should have it: "tap, turn, tap, turn."

Students may attempt a pole tap by stabbing the pole into the snow directly in front. Explain related safety concerns and reinforce proper hand, pole, and basket position. Relate pole swing to the smooth and rhythmic movement of walking with a normal arm swing. Ankle, knee, and spinal extension complement the pole swing.

You might use the clock system to further explain correct pole use. Indicate which pole is appropriate with verbal instruction or commands—"three o'clock and then nine o'clock; three o'clock and then nine o'clock," or simply "left, right, left, right." Put this in the context of the direction of the new turn: "For left turns, you'll initiate with a left pole swing and tap; for a right turn, you swing...which pole?"

Parallel Turns

- Teach initiation of open parallel turns with a pole touch. Use bumps or knolls to teach parallel initiation.
- Incorporate exercises such as the falling leaf and slipping into the fall line from a static position across the hill.

- Refine commands to include a cue for turn initiation so skiing becomes fluid and rhythmic.
- Explore long- and medium-radius parallel turns. Ski a variety of trails and conditions.
- Introduce short-radius turns on comfortable terrain.
- Refine edge- and pressure-control skills to enable them to feel carved medium- and long-radius turns.
- Introduce dynamic short-radius turns. Shorten the cadence of the command, i.e., "turn, turn, turn."
- Try slopes with small, rhythmic moguls. Before approaching the moguls, students should have experience with absorption and extension. You and the student must be competent and aggressive, with plenty of experience skiing together.
- Try new exercises and variations that include a sideslip to a hockey stop and straight running to a hockey stop.

For students who stem the skis, help them understand what stemming is and when it is occurring. Encourage downhill pole swing and edge release with a slight extension to aid the movement of center of mass downhill toward the new turn. Blind students often are reluctant to move from one stable leg until the footing for the next step is secure. Thus, many blind skiers maintain a slight stem for stability and the ability to quickly change direction if needed. An edged ski also offers more tactile feedback than a flat ski and is often used by blind skiers to understand speed, snow, and terrain conditions.

Emphasize a smooth, gradual transition from turn to turn, encouraging an earlier transfer of pressure. Describe a movement in which the knees roll together forward and laterally over the center of the skis.

ADVANCED ZONE

All of the directional commands and guiding techniques continue to apply as students with blindness or low vision move into the advanced zone. Be aware that this zone involves skiing faster, on more aggressive terrain, and in variable conditions. All of these factors force the instructor to be keenly aware of the surroundings and stay in close proximity to the student.

Teaching activities for this zone are discussed in the *Alpine Technical Manual* and can be easily adapted to a student with blindness or low vision.

Using Outriggers

chapter 5

Outriggers (or, "riggers") are probably the most widely used pieces of adaptive equipment. Outriggers can be used in all of the primary adaptive disciplines. They are most prominently used in three-track, four-track, mono-skiing, and bi-skiing.

Outriggers come in a variety of shapes and sizes. They can be carried in the hands, referred to as "hand-held," or attached to a bi-ski, commonly called "fixed" outriggers. Hand-held outriggers generally resemble forearm crutches with ski tips on the ends (see photo 5.1).

PHOTO 5.1 Hand-held Outriggers for Stand-up Skiers

Deacon Chapin Photography

By engaging a spring in the outrigger, skiers can "flip" the lower portion of the outrigger up or down into a "crutch" or "ski" position. Hence, this part of the outrigger is referred to as the "flip-ski." Standard hand-held outriggers are adjustable in height.

In many ways, outriggers are to adaptive equipment as ski poles are to standard alpine equipment. They accomplish the same purposes of timing and balance, but the outrigger serves the additional purpose of enhancing the basic control movements (edging, pressure, and rotary). Techniques for enhancing these movements and skills are discussed later.

Outrigger Sizing

To be used effectively, outriggers must fit properly. Below are recommendations for sizing the outrigger:

THREE-TRACK AND FOUR-TRACK SKIERS

Beginner/novice three-track or four-track skiers should size the outriggers for a tall, comfortable stance. Two approaches can be used:
- With the outrigger in the ski position, the handle should come to at least the greater trochanter (top of femur).

- In case of a leg-length discrepancy, the outrigger can be sized with the arms straight at the sides and through the cuffs of the outrigger. The epicondyle of the radius (the bump on the inside of the wrist) should be even with the outrigger handle.
- Size the outrigger with the student in ski boots and on skis, since this increases overall height. When in doubt, go longer rather than shorter for a beginner to avoid a stooped stance, which is tiring and makes the desired tall stance more difficult.

As students progress beyond the beginner level, they should be allowed to determine their own outrigger length based on comfort and the type of skiing intended. A good skier can still get quite low and dynamic with a longer outrigger by allowing the shoulders and elbows to rise into a soft curve or rounded arm position as the knees and ankles are flexed.

MONO-SKIERS

Beginner/novice mono-skiers should size the outriggers so that the shafts form a 35°–40° angle with the snow when in an athletic stance. A mono-skier's athletic stance can be described as follows:

- Head up and looking forward
- Shoulders, hips, and knees level
- A slight forward curvature in the spine
- Upper arms hanging vertically at the sides, with a slight space between elbows and body
- Lower arms hanging at the same angle as the outrigger shafts

When in doubt, always give a beginner longer rather than shorter outriggers. It may be necessary to screw in or remove the brake/contact bolt when sizing riggers. Reposition the brake/contact bolt as needed depending on the amount of brake or claw contact desired on the snow. Remember, tall outriggers can be harder to use in crutch position, so teach pushing and maintaining stationary position with the outrigger in a "ski" position.

BI-SKIERS

For beginners through low intermediate bi-skiers, keep the outrigger relatively short (for an adult, typically 9–12 inches from the rigger tip to the handle). This allows the skier to place the outrigger on the snow next to the hips but not farther forward than the knee unless bending forward. The bi-skier should keep the arms relatively straight, with a slight bend in the elbow and not "locked." This places the outrigger in a more powerful position for maintaining balance (closer to the hips) and effecting a "push off" cross-over movement. However, the outriggers should be long enough to

maintain contact on the snow with both outriggers while leaning 35° to one side.

Outrigger sizing for intermediate and advanced bi-skiers will be similar to that for mono-skiers. The outriggers can be lengthened as the bi-skier is introduced to more advanced rotary or steering movements and progresses to steeper terrain.

Outrigger Brake Adjustment

Adjusting the outrigger brake consists of adjusting the contact bolt or brake screw to allow for more or less articulation of the flip-ski. Less articulation of the flip-ski means that the claw at the tail of the flip-ski will be more easily engaged, making it more effective for slowing or stopping.

Adjusting the outrigger slowing or stopping will depend on your student's physical ability and general attitude. Hesitant students may need a little more brake for a sense of security. Typically, the brake should be adjusted so that the skier can propel backward on flat snow by engaging the outrigger brake/claw. The movement necessary to engage the brake will depend on the proper skiing position for the skier. Less forward torso movement is normally encouraged for a bi-skier than a mono-skier or three-tracker; consequently, bi-ski outriggers may initially be set up with more brake.

- Too Much Brake: The outriggers bounce and skip on the snow.
- Too Little Brake: The skier may have difficult controlling speed, turning effectively, or balancing due to slippage away from the skis.

Although perhaps counterintuitive, the general rule is more brake for softer snow and less for brake for firmer snow.

Using the Outrigger

The outrigger technique presented below represents the most effective cross-discipline approach currently in use. This technique is referred to as "bilateral" outrigger use, referring to the use of both outriggers. Discipline-specific modifications to this technique are described in later chapters.

This method was designed to help adaptive skiers in all of the zones—from beginner through intermediate to advanced—achieve effective skiing movements. Some additional benefits of this technique are that it:

- Creates a stable, centered stance for the beginner.
- Encourages a stable upper body, allowing the ski(s) to be guided underneath the upper body.
- Encourages keeping the shoulders, hips, and hands level through the turn, which keeps the body from tipping in.
- Assists in keeping the inside hand, shoulder, and hip leading through the turn.
- Keeps both hands in front of the body.

ROTARY MOVEMENTS

One of the most significant roles of the outrigger is to create rotary movements for turning and steering the skis. Skis are most effectively turned by a combination of muscle groups; typically, the closer these muscle groups are to the snow-ski interaction, the better.

Beginner/Novice Zone

Skiers in the beginner/novice zones use outriggers to assist in directional changes by using friction to augment whatever change they can effect by looking and pointing their bodies in the desired direction. Exceptions include skiers who can make rotary movements in the feet or legs. These skiers should be taught to create rotary movements in the feet and legs before using the outrigger to generate a turning force. Skiers who cannot generate rotary movements can use outrigger friction to stabilize the upper body and for something to turn against. Outriggers also help skiers avoid ineffective rotary movements such as initiating the turn with an abrupt or aggressive twisting of the shoulders or torso.

Before learning to turn, students should have already practiced bilateral outrigger movements: straight run exercises using both outriggers to maintain a balanced stance, braking exercises to control speed, etc. As your student begins to feel comfortable controlling the outriggers, you can introduce the outriggers to aid in turning.

- Turns across the fall line are accomplished from a gliding straight run by looking and pointing both outriggers in the direction of the turn.
- Friction is initially generated on the tail or brake of the outrigger.
- Friction is greater on the inside outrigger, creating a turning force.
- Light pressure on the outside outrigger encourages a centered stance, but care should be taken to create as little friction as possible so as not to counter the rotary effect of the inside outrigger.
- Movements during this phase should be gradual and progressive. Abrupt movements tend to disrupt the overall flow and can inhibit a balanced, centered stance. At this stage, turning the outriggers in the intended direction should be a gradual and progressive movement of the hands and wrists (photo 5.2).
- Linked turns are created as both outriggers are more actively steered in the direction of the new turn.

Brian W. Robb

- Friction continues to be generated predominantly from the brake of the outrigger, but the student is encouraged to explore friction generated from the edge of the outrigger. This may require the brake screw to be slightly shortened.
- Friction continues to be greater on the inside outrigger.
- More active steering of the outriggers implies that both outriggers move in the direction of the turn, thus moving arms and shoulders toward the turn.
- Although both outriggers are steered in the direction of the turn, the inside shoulder, hand, and outrigger lead, reducing shoulder rotation and oversteering.
- Light pressure on the outside outrigger helps maintain a centered stance.

Intermediate Zone
- Intermediate to advanced linked turns are accomplished with an increased focus on the inside outrigger and less reliance on friction to initiate turns.
- Friction is now generated from the edge of the outrigger, requiring that the brake screw continue to be shortened or removed.

- The inside outrigger is actively steered in the direction of the turn.
- The outrigger movement is similar to a pole swing movement in terms of timing, direction, and intensity.
- Inside outrigger friction at turn initiation is light and momentary.
- Friction movements are enhanced by a counter motion of the upper and lower body, thus placing the skier in an anticipated and countered position.
- Outside outrigger pressure discourages the skier from banking with the head and shoulders. Outside outrigger pressure occurs primarily during the latter portion of the turn, orienting pressure to the outside and directing movement downhill.

Effective cross-over movements are critical at this stage. To accomplish these, the skier's head, shoulders, arms, and outriggers are directed toward the center of the turn. This flattens the skis and shifts pressure toward the inside outrigger.

Advanced Zone
At this stage, the skier moves aggressively into the turn with the upper body and outriggers (see photo 5.2). This cross-over move

puts the skis on edge early, enabling a carved turn. Outriggers should have little brake to reduce rotary movements and skidding.

In the advanced zone, skiers continue to refine movements to adjust for a variety of snow conditions and terrain. Short-radius and rotary-dominant turns provide versatility and are accomplished with strong friction on the inside outrigger.

- Turn the outrigger perpendicular to the ski, creating friction with the entire edge.
- Use outriggers and muscle tension to keep the upper body pointed down the fall line.
- Exaggerate extension and flexion in a lateral forward manner to weight and unweight the skis.
- Reduce pressure/friction on the outside outrigger.

EDGING MOVEMENTS

Outriggers can also be used to make edging movements. Pushing the outriggers against the snow one at a time can move the skier's center of mass laterally to create inclination. Inclination is a strong form of edging movement that allows the skier to remain skeletally aligned and withstand greater forces in a turn. For instance, a bi-skier may use a "Hip Drop Wing Block Technique" by creating a lateral thrust as a result of pushing off with one outrigger, followed by an upward thrust with the other outrigger to keep the inside shoulder high and create angles at the hips and spine (photo 5.3).

By projecting one or both outriggers in the direction of a turn, a skier can draw the center of mass into the turn and create a strong cross-over movement.

PHOTO 5.3 A bi-skier keeps the inside shoulder high through outrigger support.

Brian W. Robb

PRESSURING MOVEMENTS

Outriggers can assist a skier in distributing weight to different parts of the skis: laterally, fore- aft, and weight-unweight. Because outriggers have considerable weight, slight shifts in their position can change the center of mass significantly. This is amplified because the weight of the outrigger is away from the skier's center of mass. For example, the center of mass can be shifted fore and aft by sliding the outriggers fore and aft. Extending one outrigger farther from the body while pulling the other one in will shift weight to the side.

Lateral (side-to-side) pressuring movements can also be achieved by pushing against the snow with one outrigger at a time. Combining an extension of one outrigger away from the body with a pressuring movement (pushing off) with the other outrigger can create very strong and quick lateral weight transfer to the side.

A skier can weight or unweight the skis by rapidly raising or lowering the outriggers. This technique is sometimes used by skiers in deep powder. Unweighting can also be accomplished by pushing straight down on the snow with one or both outriggers.

A skier can initiate a turn in powder by rapidly throwing the outside outrigger upward and into the direction of the turn. This movement has the dual effect of unweighting the ski and creating upper body rotation.

ENHANCING BALANCE

Outriggers help a skier maintain balance in at least two ways:

1. Outriggers provide a direct link to the snow. This enables the skier to dynamically relocate the center of mass, and thus maintain balance, by pushing against the snow. The additional sensory input can also aid in balance.
2. Outriggers add mass to the skier's arms, allowing the skier to shift balance with subtle movements away from or toward the center of mass—just as a tightrope artist uses a pole to aid balance.

These outrigger uses are not intended to be all-inclusive; they illustrate ways in which outrigger movements assist skiers in effectively maintaining balance, turning, edging, and pressuring the skis.

As you teach students to use outriggers, encourage the following:

- Focus on gliding, not braking.
- Move the center of mass in the direction of the new turn.
- Eliminate inefficient rotary movements at turn initiation.

Equipment and Stance for Stand-up Skiers

chapter 6

Adaptive equipment is one of the key reasons that adaptive skiing is a separate discipline within PSIA and what makes skiing possible for so many individuals. A thorough knowledge of adaptive equipment and its use is critical for a safe and enjoyable skiing experience. Consider the following guidelines in helping your adaptive student get started.

Clothing

Clothes should be functional and appropriate for the weather conditions and, ideally, allow the student to "fit in with the skiing crowd." Students who skied before their injury or illness may already have suitable clothing, but newcomers to the sport may not. Some adaptive ski programs have items available to lend. If yours does not, you may want to build up your own loaner inventory or locate a store in the area that will rent clothing for the day.

Equipment

Of course, this is a prime concern. Check to see that the boots fit properly, have a soft flex, and are on the right feet. Check that skis are the correct length and model. Lighter weight equipment can be helpful. Make note of any outdated, inappropriate, or unsafe equipment the student may bring to the lesson and encourage a trip to a local rental shop to obtain proper and safe gear.

Always familiarize new skiers with the basics of ski equipment: how the boot fits into the binding, how the bindings work, why the skis are shaped as they are, and what the poles are for. Show the student how to carry the equipment and where to store it when not in use. For young skiers, consider taping their name on the equipment to make it easier to find and retrieve.

Developing a Skiing Stance

Proper equipment helps the student achieve a balanced, functional, athletic stance while skiing. An athletic stance is described in the *Level I Study Guide* (PSIA 1996) as follows: "This is a fairly tall stance in which the weight is balanced equally over both feet, with the ankles, knees, hips and spine bent forward slightly. The upper body is upright but relaxed; the hands are comfortably ahead within the peripheral vision. The hips and upper body are centered over the feet. Viewed from the side, the head and shoulders appear to be 'stacked' over the hips and feet."

One cause of an impaired stance is lack of muscle tone, which often translates to an inability to bend the stiff ski boot through ankle flex. This results in a "sit-back" stance, in which the back of the leg rests against the back of the ski boot, contributing to a wedge that is over-edged and with the tips too far apart.

Although this sit-back stance might appear balanced and comfortable, it can retard the skill development necessary for parallel skiing by making it impossible to guide the ski from the mid-foot. This prevents the skis from flattening, the inside foot from guiding simultaneously with the outside foot on corresponding edges, and the center of mass from flowing into the next turn.

Impaired stance may have other anatomical causes such as overly pronated or supinated feet, musculoskeletal imbalances, and bone or joint deformities. Adaptive instructors are often called upon to adjust the student's equipment to help improve the stance, primarily using in-the-boot adjustments that provide padding or support. More extensive technical adjustments are beyond the training of most instructors and warrant referral to a professional boot fitter or binding technician. You can be a resource for your student by being aware of equipment needs, devising solutions, and developing relationships with local providers who can tailor equipment and adjustments to suit your students' situation.

START WITH THE FEET

Begin by checking the student's regular shoes for differential wear, and then by observing the gait and stance from behind. Is the student severely bow-legged or knock-kneed? Do the feet move through a normal heel-to-toe motion? Is the footstrike on one side significantly different from the other side? If possible, have the student stand in a natural stance and use plywood blocks or various pads to fill in the gaps and determine the amount of non-corrective canting needed to create equalized pressure on both sides of the foot.

"Filling the gap" is a type of non-corrective canting that helps the skier transmit pressure and/or movements to the whole sole of the boot but does not change the skier's natural body position. It's not used to adjust body or foot position. It could be helpful for a condition such as spastic cerebral palsy, in which the spasticity can cause excessive pronation.

An adaptive instructor can take certain actions to modify ill-fitting boots or help the student compensate for excessive pronation, supination, or even leg-length differences. You can also use canting to address a need for heel or toe lifts, although as a general rule you should start with no more than a half-inch of non-corrective canting inside the boots. Too much canting can alter the boot's fit and make it uncomfortable. If more canting is needed and would not compromise comfort, it can be added incrementally.

LEG-LENGTH ASSESSMENT

A difference in leg length may affect the stance of your student. Techniques for assessing leg length are easy to perform (see photo 6.1). As the student sits on a bench with back and buttocks firmly against a wall and feet firmly on the floor, place your thumbs at the bottom of the student's kneecaps. If you see no obvious leg-length difference (i.e., your thumbs are at the same height), have the student extend both legs while you gently cup the heels. Are your hands even?

Another method is to for the student to stand with the feet at shoulder width with the heels, buttocks, and back firmly against a wall but with the knees slightly flexed. Use small plywood blocks in $\frac{1}{4}$-, $\frac{1}{2}$-, $\frac{3}{4}$-, and 1-inch increments (see photo 6.2). If one leg is obviously shorter than the other or the hip bones are obviously not level, place the blocks in increasing increments under the foot of the shorter leg until the hips become level. This can be determined visually or with a tape measure.

PHOTO 6.1 Checking for Leg-length Difference

Deacon Chapin Photography

PHOTO 6.2 Leg-length Assessment using Blocks

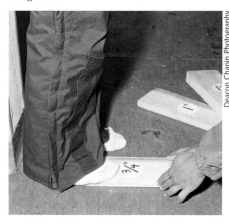

Deacon Chapin Photography

PHOTO 6.3 Boot-fitting Materials

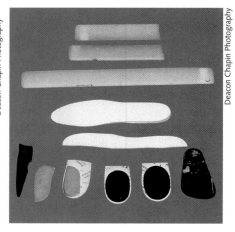

Deacon Chapin Photography

Adjusting the Equipment

BOOTS

Now that you have assessed and observed your student's stance, you are prepared to make the necessary adjustments to equipment. Start by pulling the liner from the boot and adding material where needed; a variety of cants, lifts, footbeds, or foam padding are available from ski shops or shoe repair shops, as shown in photo 6.3. You may need to turn these materials or cut them in half to accommodate the fitting.

Cants are placed on the outside half of the foot for students who pronate (i.e., rotate inward or bear weight mostly on the medial side of the foot), or to the inside half of the foot for students who supinate (i.e., rotate outward or bear weight mostly on the lateral side of the boot). The goal is for the skier to be supported in a natural stance and have the ski run flat on the snow. This is an example of non-corrective canting.

Use straight lifts to compensate for leg-length discrepancies. These are cut to fit the whole length of the foot and taped to the boot liner (duct tape is handy for this). The general rule is to use $1/4$-inch less than the leg-length difference, because the student has probably learned to compensate naturally to some degree.

Use heel lifts to help a skier whose weight is naturally too far back on the ski (aft pressure). Skiers with cerebral palsy may experience this due to weak quadriceps (thighs). Below-the-knee amputees with little to no ankle flex might also need a heel lift.

Use toe lifts to help a skier whose weight is too far forward (fore pressure), such as skiers with spina bifida who use long leg braces. The braces make it difficult to flex the ankles or knees, forcing the center of mass forward.

FLEX AND FIT

As you work with the student's boots, be sure to assess flex and overall fit. Weaker or lighter weight skiers often are hampered by boots that are too stiff. Loosening buckles and removing shims can help, as may wearing thinner socks. If these measures do not work the student may have to take the boots to a professional fitter or, alternatively, rent a lighter, more flexible pair.

SLANT BOARD

Students with disabilities associated with extreme leg-length discrepencies (e.g., post-polio), extreme supination or pronation (e.g., spastic cerebral palsy), or the inability to apply pressure the front of back of the ski (e.g., a disability requiring long leg braces) are good candidates for slant boards. A slant board consists of a binding mounted on top of a board, which is then mounted to a ski by use of a ball and pinion joint. A certified binding technician must make the fitting, but you can learn to make minor adjustments to the slant board (up-down, side-to-side, and fore-aft) with Allen wrenches.

Ski Selection and Modification

Appropriate ski length is determined by weighing many factors, including the student's height and weight, general physical condition, range of motion, strength, skiing experience, and proficiency. Obviously, a beginner/novice skier does not need high-end racing skis, and an advanced racer will find recreational skis inadequate. As a tool to help achieve a student's goals, the skis should be stable and easy to turn, regardless of the student's ability. In general, rental shop recommendations for able-bodied skiers also meet the needs of adaptive skiers.

Many new types of skis have become available for able-bodied skiers (e.g. shaped skis, short skis, and ski blades). These can be great tools for the adaptive instructor and students as well. Care should be used when choosing a ski style for your student. Qualified technicians can make adjustments to fine-tune a ski for the skier's needs. For example, correct alignment can be achieved by inserting fiberglass shims under the binding. This adjustment is a type of canting that is corrective, i.e., it changes the skier's natural stance. The goal is to have the ski rest flat on the snow with weight distributed evenly along the its length.

Adaptive Equipment Options

A complete and detailed student analysis is needed to determine if the student is a stand-up skier. Review physical strength and range of motion (e.g., strength of limbs, ability to balance, and ability to move or lean left/right) as well as cognitive strengths and weakness. This evaluation will determine the equipment needed to create a successful learning environment.

Many types of adaptive equipment are currently in use. These range from a simple bamboo pole to an elaborate articulating walker. Many adaptive stand-up skiers do not need adaptive equipment, while others may need multiple adaptations. The following is a list of some common pieces of adaptive equipment and a brief description of each:

- **Walker**—An adjustable hospital walker with skis attached, used for students with severe balance problems who cannot totally support themselves. Recommended height is level with the person's hips. Usually requires two instructors to assist a student when using the walker.

- **Ski leg/snow slider**—Similar to a walker with skis but with articulating joints, including an adjustment for edge angle (photo 6.4).
- **Ski blocks**—Installed near the tip of the skis to prevent crossing.
- **Ski bra**—A hook-and-eye assembly that screws to the tips of the skis to prevent tips from crossing but does allows a parallel or wedge position. Generally used if the skier has decreased lateral control of one or both legs. Exercise caution concerning the potential for sliding backwards. Three variations are: J's (hook-and-eye system easily disconnects), S's (hook-and-eye system is secure), and trombone sliders (allow the student to shuffle the skis forward or backward but are heavier than a regular ski-bra).
- **Edgie-Wedgie**—A lightweight, 6-inch piece of rubber tubing with a small clamp and thumbscrew at each end that holds the tips together loosely but does not prevent crossing.
- **Ski clip**—Similar to an edgie-wedgie but uses cotton cord instead of rubber and has a length adjustment.
- **Ski bungee**—A permanent type of ski-bra system in which holes are drilled through the tips of the skis to attach a heavy bungee cord or chain to keep the tips together.
- **Outriggers**—Forearm crutches with a regular or lightweight ski tip mounted at the base. String/spring mechanism allows the ski tip to flip up for better stability when walking. Outriggers come in many different sizes and adjustable.

- **Tether reins**—Straps attached to ski-bra system with a carabiner or steel triangle and that are controlled by the skier's arms to affect turn shape and speed.
- **Harness system**—Strap device that goes around the skier's hips or waist with tethers on each side to allow the instructor to control turn shape and speed.
- **Seizure/retention strap**—Strap device (e.g., a climbing harness) that goes around the skier's chest or waist and attaches to the chairlift to prevent the skier from falling off in the event of case of a seizure. Sometimes used for students that are difficult to control on the lift.
- **Slant board**—A board mounted with a binding that has an adjustable base to raise or lower the toe or heel or to compensate for exces-sive pronation or supination. Used to bring the skier as close as possible to level without changing the skier's stance; maximum adjustment is usually about 4 inches.
- **Mono-board/mono-ski**—A short, double-width ski (approximately 8 inches wide) with two bindings mounted side-by-side in the center. Although not designed as an adaptive skiing tool, mono-boards are well suited for some four-track skiers who wear full leg braces with fixed hinges and for skiers with fused joints.
- **FM system**—One-way radio communication system consisting of a transmitter (worn by the instructor) and receiver (worn by the student) to aid in verbal commands. Used primarily for students who are vision- or hearing impaired or have an attention-deficit disorder.

PHOTO 6.4 Ski Legs

Brian W. Robb

- **Skier bib**—Worn by students with visual or hearing impairments and their guides to alert other skiers and riders on the mountain.
- **Duct tape**—One of the most versatile pieces of adaptive equipment available to the instructor.

Physical Assists for Stand-up Skiers

Physical assists are sometimes necessary for the adaptive skier; a few are described below:

- **Single short pole assist**—Short bamboo pole held at waist or shoulder height by both student and instructor. Instructor skis backwards.
- **Single long pole assist**—Single bamboo pole held at waist or chest height. Instructor and student ski beside each other.
- **Horse and buggy**—Two poles, one in each hand of student and instructor, held at hip height. One person skis in front, the other immediately in back.

- **Clam shell**—Two heavy, strong bamboo poles (or lighter poles taped together) held by two instructors; one pole is placed below the student's buttocks, the other placed at waist or chest height for the student's hands.
- **Hula Hoop™**—The instructor and student hold on to the Hula Hoop™ while the instructor skis backwards. The advantage of this assist is that the student must stand up and cannot lean against the hula hoop.
- **Two-point hold**—The instructor is behind the student and places one ski between the student's skis and one on the outside of the student's skis. The instructor places one hand above or below the student's knee and the other hand on the student's shoulder or hip (photo 6.5). By gently moving the leg and hip, the instructor can assist the student in turning and stopping.

- **Ski pole/ski bra assist**—The strap of one of the instructor's ski poles is attached to the ski bra. The instructor then skis backwards holding the ski pole while leading the student.

Conclusion

Determining the appropriate equipment for your student and adjusting it properly will to a large extent determine the success of the lesson. The information provided here should give you many options. This undertaking is challenging and can be costly in terms of time and, sometimes, money. However, proper outfitting is key to your student's comfort and ability to move efficiently. Even if progress seems slow, be patient; success is the reward for persistence.

PHOTO 6.5 Two-point Hold

Deacon Chapin Photography

Three-track Skiing

chapter 7

This chapter provides more specific information for three-track skier assessment, instruction, and equipment, including exercises for beginner/novice, intermediate, and advanced zones. You can build on this information by using each interaction with your students as an opportunity for research into what works best for different situations. The goal is to develop a broad enough understanding of tools and techniques to be able to meet each student's physical and mental needs. The following will help guide you in this process.

PHOTO 7.1 Three-track Skiing

Brian W. Robb

Definition of Three-track Skiing

Three-track skiing is skiing on one ski while using outriggers to maintain balance. Note the purposeful statement "skiing on one ski" instead of "skiing on one leg." It is not uncommon for a student who is a bilateral amputee to ski with a prosthesis on one leg.

Many disabilities affect the strength, reflexes, and range of motion of one leg or the other, predisposing a skier for three-track skiing. Diseases and accidents may also take their toll on a skier's ability to ski on two legs. A few examples are developmental or muscular diseases that affect one leg, rods or pins in a badly broken leg, a severe knee injury, fused ankles, or a traumatic accident that leaves one leg weak or non-functioning.

With or without a sound leg, the three-track student is able to stand on one ski and maintain dynamic balance with the assistance of outriggers. Whether the student needs outriggers designed for children or adults, all models provide a range of lengths and adjustments. Arm cuff styles and materials also vary. Most are plastic or metal with openings to the side, and many models have Velcro™ straps to help secure the arm. Modifications to the handles may include padding for comfort or to increase diameter for a better grip. Outrigger ski tips range from discarded ski tips to lightweight, molded plastic tips. Materials used for the outriggers determine their weight; heavier ones are more stable for beginners, while lighter ones are ideal for racers.

Assessment Specific to Three-Track Skiers

- Is there an obvious amputation? If not, what is the condition of the legs? A simple review with the student will determine whether two-track or three-track skiing is more appropriate—i.e., whether the student bears weight on one or both legs.

- For students with an amputation, what is the type and location of the amputation? The partial or complete removal of a body limb affects the student's ability to balance, initiate rotational forces, and pressure and edge a ski.

- Were there any complications during or after the surgery? Healing may be slow and indicate circulation problems or other items to be considered, such as diabetes or skin/tissue pressure problems.

- How long ago was the limb amputated? Ample time, usually 6 to 12 months, needs to elapse for tissues to heal, circulation to stabilize, and the limb to desensitize to heat and cold. Generally, the student will have been informed of an appropriate schedule by the doctor.
- What was the cause of the amputation and is the student on medications? Knowing the origins of the disability and use of medications provides information relative to sensitivity to cold or sunlight, strength and energy levels, susceptibility to fatigue, and so forth. Knowing if the amputation is organic or traumatic in nature provides additional information about the student's overall physical and psychological condition.
- Does the below-the-knee (BK) or the above-the-knee (AK) amputee's gait exhibit one of the following?
  - Excessive bending of the trunk—may indicate balance problems.
  - A wide stance—may indicate balance problems and/or a bilateral amputation.
  - A rotational or swing-though movement of the prosthesis when stepping—may indicate a locked knee or a prosthesis that is too long.
  - Rising onto the toe of the sound foot—may indicate an inability to flex the prosthesis at either the knee or ankle.
  - A prominent toe or heel strike with the dominantly weighted foot—may indicate that the student will predominantly pressure the front or back of the ski.
  - Pronation or supination of the dominantly weighted foot—may indicate inability to maintain a flat ski.

- Is the student walking or using crutches? Crutch use indicates some strength in the upper body and/or a lack of ability to place weight on the prosthesis.
- When conducting the "hands on" assessment of the student's ability to move, what are your findings in the following areas?
  - Ability to rotate their leg(s)—may indicate their ability to steer their ski(s).
  - Ability to abduct (draw the limb away from the midline) or adduct (draw the limb toward the midline) the leg(s) while standing—may indicate the amount of independent leg action.
  - Amount of ankle flexion—may indicate ability to maintain balance and initiate pressure and edging movements. If flexion is absent, insert heel wedges inside the boot's bladder or between the bladder and shell to help the student pressure the front of the boot and ski tip.
  - Range of motion and strength of the arm(s) and hand(s)—may indicate the ability to grasp the pole(s) or the outrigger(s) and move the upper torso to enhance balance, timing, and turn initiation.
  - Range of motion and flexibility of the trunk while in a balanced stance—may indicate the ability to move fore and aft and side to side to create dynamic balance.
- To what degree does the student feel pain, heat, or cold in a residual limb and/or all limbs? Generally, the circulation and sensitivity of a residual limb is much less than that of a normal limb. It is quite possible for an amputee to get frostbite or have pressure points or sores without knowing it. If the

amputation is due to diabetes, the circulation is generally poor in all limbs. In addition, some medications affect the sensitivity of the extremities.
- Does the student wear foot or leg braces? The student may need a larger boot to accommodate a brace. You may need to insert padding to eliminate extra space and prevent pressure points where the brace rubs against the leg. In some cases, a ski boot may provide as much support as a foot brace. For students with a long leg brace, consider how they might be able to ride the chairlift.
- Does the student stand flat in the ski boot? If not, you may need to realign the shaft of the boot cuff or introduce canting.

The information you gain through a thorough student assessment will provide insight into student abilities, goals, and needs. The following scenarios illustrate some likely conclusions you could draw to help shape your lesson.

SCENARIO #1

Ashley is a 35-year-old bilateral below-knee amputee who also has weakness in her arms. Her residual limbs are 8 inches and 4 inches long. The 8-inch limb has a prosthesis with a dorsiplantar (up-down) flexing ankle, and Ashley has limited strength and ability to grasp in the corresponding arm and hand. She also has a prosthesis for the 4-inch limb, but it does not have a flexing ankle.

Teaching tactic: The 8-inch residual limb with its prosthesis is the strongest and most capable "leg" to use in skiing. Because Ashley already has a dorsiplantar flexing ankle, she probably does not require heel wedges in the boot bladder to enable her to pressure the cuff of the boot and the ski tip. However, you will need to check the alignment of the prosthesis in the boot and assess whether she requires boot canting to ensure full contact with the cuff.

Although the 4-inch stump has a prosthesis to aid walking, the torque and pressure applied by a boot and ski can initiate unwanted rotation and cause undue pressure on the stump. An exception would be if Ashley were equipped with an extremely well-fitting, custom ski leg. Therefore, the 4-inch stump could be fully protected against cold and impact and the prosthesis for that leg left in the locker room. Alternatively, Ashley could ski wearing the prosthesis with a street shoe. If she could actively keep the leg with the short prosthesis out of the way while skiing, it may provide the welcome ability to rest between runs by standing on both legs.

The weak upper limbs and limited grasp strength demands that Ashley use lightweight outriggers. The outriggers should be somewhat long to provide Ashley with the maximum ability to balance on her skeletal frame, including the one prosthesis. Determine whether she can adequately grasp the handles of the outriggers. If not, have her use Velcro™ straps to enhance grip strength.

SCENARIO #2

Gregor is a 50-year-old man with bilateral above-knee and below-elbow amputations. He is in good shape and trains regularly at the gym.

Teaching tactic: With bilateral amputations, a balanced stance is possible. The strength of the skiing leg compensates for the lack of an outrigger on that side, and the arm using the outrigger helps compensate for the leg amputation. A student must be strong and well conditioned to do this. As always, you will need to conduct a complete review that addresses how the foot fits into the boot, how the cuff fits, and Gregor's ability to pressure, steer, etc. Boot and binding adjustments may increase is ability to achieve dynamic balance and apply rotary force.

Equipment Selection and Set-up

Selection and modification of boots and skis are integral to skier performance. See Chapter 6 for information on selecting boots and skis and achieving an athletic stance.

Fatigue levels are generally higher for three-track students who walk without crutches or exercise their upper bodies than for students who use a prosthesis. Having the student walk in the ski boot with outriggers during dryland practice provides a good indication of whether fatigue is likely to be an issue. This also allows the student to become accustomed to the boot and outriggers before attempting to use them on a slippery surface.

Three-track skiers can benefit from many of the same types of adaptive equipment used by four-track skiers—e.g., tethers and slant boards. See Chapter 6 for more information on these items.

Teaching Information

When establishing a lesson plan, the comprehensive student evaluation provides necessary information about the student's strengths and can outline some areas of concern. This information, coupled with student input on personal goals and concerns about skiing, forms the basis of the learning partnership between you and your student.

Three-track skiers are capable of developing all of the basic movement skills of skiing, although you will need to modify the standard exercise progression somewhat. Developing the balancing skill will be a significant challenge for most three-trackers, but once basic skills are established, development is similar to that of two-trackers.

Many two-track exercises can also be used for three-track. You can develop new exercises by modifying those found in PSIA-AASI materials. *The Alpine Handbook* (PSIA 1996) contains a wealth of exercises to serve as a starting point for your progressions. Stress safety and the appropriate use of terrain when developing exercises.

BEGINNER/NOVICE ZONE

Your first challenge will be to help the student attain a balanced stance while minimizing fatigue. A standard ski progression (introduction to equipment, walking and sliding, step-turning on the flats, side stepping, straight running, etc.) should be pursued while carefully monitoring energy level. Using the outriggers in the crutch position (tips perpendicular to the snow) enhances balance while walking. Outriggers need to be returned to the ski position (tips sliding on the snow) when attempting to glide.

You can help reduce fatigue by:
- taking frequent rests by sitting on the snow or in a chair,
- pushing the student up the slope (with permission), and
- taking a break and to get some food or drink.

Skiing is meant to be fun, so remember that moving around on the flats can be extremely hard for a three-track skier!

As with any student, pay attention to basic athletic stance. An upright, flexed position (not bent at the waist) with outriggers positioned ahead of the toe binding area is desirable. An outrigger that is too short will force the student to bend at the waist, which shifts weight to the heel and applies little or no pressure to the boot tongue. After checking outrigger length, use the same corrective stance and balance exercises as for a two-track skier. A flat ski is desired in all straight run exercises. You may need to help adjust the equipment prior to each practice run.

Students will probably need assistance after a fall. Have them position the ski downhill and across the slope and push up with an outrigger. On the first attempt, help by placing your boot/ski against theirs and gently pull them to an upright position. For safety, reiterate the importance of getting the outriggers away from the body during a fall.

Typically, the side opposite the impaired leg is stronger. A good motto when teaching adaptive students is to "utilize strengths and overcome weaknesses." When teaching the side step, have students face so the leg/ski is on the downhill side, with the residual limb/non-ski side uphill. When teaching students to turn, have the first turn be toward the side without the ski.

Introduction to Equipment
Explain equipment function, setup, and proper use. Demonstrate how outriggers work in the up (crutch) and down (skiing) positions and explain the function of the outrigger brakes. Then, give the student time to practice.

Flatland Drills and Exercises
- Practice getting in and out of bindings.
- Engage in a game of "follow-the-leader" to gain experience moving on the flats.
- Practice lifting one outrigger at a time, balancing on the ski.
- Demonstrate how the outriggers can be used for slowing and stopping.
- Monitor the student's energy level; moving around on the flats can be very tiring for a beginner/novice three-tracker. You can help reduce fatigue by taking rest stops, such as sitting on the snow or a bench and getting food or drink. You also can help by pushing the student uphill—with permission.
- Make sure that outrigger length is adjusted for a tall, comfortable stance.

Sliding and Gliding, Straight Run Exercises
- Start from a bullfighter stance on a slight grade (i.e., use the outriggers for support and step the tail of the ski around until the student is facing down the fall line). Flip the outriggers into the skiing position and glide down the slope to a terrain-assisted stop.
- Develop balancing skills by alternately lifting the outriggers off the snow.
- If balancing skills and self-confidence warrant, lift both outriggers off the snow at once.
- Practice pressure movements by flexing or extending, performing fore or aft movements, and hopping while in a straight run.
- Practice stopping by pushing the outriggers to the tip of the ski, then engaging the claws on the outrigger's tail. The student will

need to increase the angles in the ankle, knee, and waist. Emphasize the benefits of flexing the ankle and knee (e.g., sinking versus bending at the waist).
- Starting from a straight run position (with chin and head pointing straight ahead), steer the ski slightly to the left, then the right, while maintaining a flat ski. It helps at this point if you ski in front, in an inverted wedge position, to keep the student focused on body alignment and steering only by moving the foot.
- Promote the feeling of steering and letting the ski skid by encouraging static exercises on the flats, such as "brushing the tail of the ski," while remaining balanced on the outriggers.
- Initiate the first turn by steering (pointing) the ski in one direction until coming to a stop, then steer the ski in the other direction to a stop. By pointing the ski, foot, leg, or hip and keeping the ski flat, the student should be able to change direction. Turn completion can be enhanced by selecting terrain that facilitates skidding. An area with a little bit of pitch with terrain rolls in it would be perfect.

Students who are watching their feet can exert pressure on the heel due to bending at the waist. Ask the student to "look ahead" to help maintain an upright stance.

Edging during a straight run may indicate that (1) the student finds it difficult to balance, (2) the boot is too loose, (3) the terrain is too steep, or (4) the student is anxious and wants to slow down or stop. Address the importance of a flat ski. Continued edging may indicate the need for canting.

First Turns and Linking Turns

- From a straight run, steer the ski in one direction to a stop (typically to the affected side first).
- Steer the ski in the opposite direction and come to a stop.
- Encourage increased steering movements in the foot and leg to enhance turn shape.
- Practice steering slightly in and out of the fall line.
- Gradually increase the diameter of the turn (from slight, snake-like, steered turns to more C-shaped turns) to control speed and changes in direction.
- Experiment with extension and flexion movements throughout the turn.

The ultimate goal is for the student to use the foot and leg to steer the ski in both directions. If this fails, encourage the use of the outriggers to assist turning (see Chapter 5).

Once a three-track skier feels comfortable with balance, linking turns comes quickly. Make sure you give the student ample ski time before moving on to other skills.

Riding the Chairlift

Teach how to ride the chairlift safely, with the outriggers in the correct position for loading and riding the lift. The student negotiates the lift line and gets ready to load with the outriggers in the crutch position, then flips the outriggers to the ski position and sits in the chair when it touches the back of the leg (see photo 7.2). Loading the chair with the outriggers in the crutch position can cause them to catch on the snow, leading to a fall. After loading, the student raises the outriggers off the snow and slides back into the chair.

Have the student prepare for unloading by sitting upright with the outriggers (still in the ski position)

PHOTO 7.2 Load the chair with outriggers in the ski position.

Deacon Chapin Photography

parallel to the unloading ramp. When the ski contacts the ramp, the student stands up, places the outriggers on the snow, and skis off.

INTERMEDIATE ZONE
Enhancing Cross-over

- Traverse small bumps to further develop absorption and extension.
- Do exercises that encourage moving down the hill and in the direction of the turn (e.g., garlands and initiation/extension exercises).
- "Hop" the tail or whole ski while initiating a turn. This illustrates the importance of movement towards the turn. This exercise also requires the student to find a comfortable, centered stance.
- Initiate a turn with a small hop. Hopping a traverse (such as with the thousand-steps exercise outlined in the *Alpine Handbook*) can be fatiguing, so perform this exercise in small doses.
- Practice the falling-leaf exercise. This is an edging, balancing, and pressuring exercise all in one!
- Increase awareness of the relationship between body weight and distribution of weight over the ski by applying extreme pressure on the front and then the back of the boot cuff.
- Encourage proper outrigger movements in which the student steers both outriggers in the direction of the turn. This directs the upper body toward the turn and helps initiate the turn.

- Keep the outriggers parallel to the edges of the slope and ski with a pendulum motion in which the leg goes from turn to turn under the trunk (cross under).
- Focus on racking up the miles and experiencing varied terrain.

In the intermediate phase, skill development continues to be similar to that of two-track skiers. Outriggers become more and more like ski poles, so this is a good time to introduce the principles of ski pole use, including timing and balance.

Continue to help focus on progressive edging, extending in the direction of the turn, having the outrigger position coincide with extension to draw the body into the turn (see photo 7.3), controlling speed, and learning to ski more of the mountain.

ADVANCED ZONE

At this level, let the mountain be both the teacher and the playground!
- Students can improve overall skiing skills by running gates, playing in the terrain park or halfpipe, and skiing a variety of snow conditions and terrain.
- Incorporate exercises that focus on skill blending.

Skiing varied terrain and at higher speeds creates many new challenges for the student. A common problem for many three-trackers is "breaking at the waist," which causes the upper torso to dart forward and the weight to shift to the heel. Focus on keeping a tall, athletic stance and using the knee as a shock absorber. Encourage applying pressure to the boot cuff or pressing down on the ski.

Enjoy this opportunity to explore the mountain together. If appropriate, challenge yourself by skiing with outriggers and one ski just like the student. Most of all, be safe and have fun!

PHOTO 7.3 The outrigger position coincides with body extension.

Brian W. Robb

Four-track Skiing

chapter 8

This chapter covers all aspects of four-track skiing, including different four-track techniques, and associated equipment features and their benefits. It also details skier evaluation guidelines, how to determine the proper adaptive equipment, and which movement patterns to emphasize in the developmental progression. As with most disciplines, experience is the best way to become familiar with the wide range of four-track skiers and equipment modifications.

The chapter provides three different skiing progressions to accommodate students who would best benefit from wedge, parallel, or walker apparatus techniques.

Definition of Four-track Skiing

Candidates for four-track skiing have a mobility challenge that requires them to use outriggers or a walker apparatus for stability due to balance problems or general weakness in the legs. Most utilize four points of contact with the snow (i.e., two skis and two outriggers or two skis with a walker). The skis may be connected with a ski bra at the tips and sometimes with a spacer bar between the feet, or the skis may need to be connected to a walker on skis for additional stability. Some four-track skiers successfully ski on a monoboard with outriggers. Potential users of this apparatus include those with severe hip problems or full leg braces and high-bilateral amputees who use prostheses.

Outriggers serve four basic functions: they aid balance, propulsion, slowing, and turning. The position of the feet and legs in snowboarding may make it a good alternative to four-track skiing for some students (see Chapter 12).

Assessment Specific to Four-Track Skiers

- Does the student walk independently or use a cane, crutches, walker, or wheelchair? It is important to determine the student's mobility. A four-tracker must have the balance, strength, and mobility to move on skis while standing. Balance aids may include:
  - ◗ one or two outriggers for people who walk without assistive devices or use only a single cane or crutch,
  - ◗ two outriggers for people who walk with two canes or two crutches, and
  - ◗ two outriggers or a walker apparatus for people who use a walker or wheelchair.

Remember that many four-trackers walk without a cane or crutches but use one or two outriggers to

PHOTO 8.1 Four-track Skiing

Brian W. Robb

improve their dynamic balance or turn initiation while skiing. Some users of manual or electric powered wheelchairs choose to stand to ski. Use safety and the student's goals as a guide for determining the appropriate equipment and your teaching approach.

■ Can the student stand for extended periods and maintain a balanced position on flat skis? If not, adaptive equipment such as wedges, cants, heel wedges, a slant board, or having the bindings mounted fore or aft of the center mark may help. Having a chair or bench nearby to periodically rest upon throughout beginner/novice lessons or when standing for any length of time can also be beneficial. See Chapter 6 for information about these adjustments.

■ Does the student have a swing-through gait, a scissors gait, or use a walker? Evaluating gait will help you choose between outriggers and a walker apparatus and adjusting your teaching progression. For example:

  ▸ A scissors and independent gait may indicate the ability to ski in a wedge (see the **wedge progression** in this chapter).

  ▸ A swing-through gait may indicate inability to ski in a wedge. If so, begin by teaching parallel movements (see the **parallel progression** in this chapter).

  ▸ Use of a walker generally indicates the need to ski with a walker apparatus (see the **walker progression** in this chapter).

■ Can the student move each leg out to the side and bring it back to a neutral stance position (abduction/adduction)? Inability to move the legs laterally may be helped by a ski bra, spacer bar, or tether and generally indicates use of a parallel progression.

Equipment Selection and Setup

Your challenge early on is to equip your student appropriately. Whether the process is quick and easy or takes a few lessons, proper equipment and setup is essential for eventual success. When choosing equipment, the primary factors that drive your decision are the student's strength, balance (fore/aft and lateral), and stance. The goal is to help the student start out with a balanced position over the center of the ski.

To enhance turning ability, consider shaped or all-mountain skis. If the student needs leg braces to stand erect, ensure that the braces fit comfortably without pinching and that no metal is exposed. With short braces (i.e., an ankle foot orthosis, or AFO brace), the boot provides important support, so you will need to be sure that it fits well and is properly buckled. Any corrective measures to help maintain a balanced stance (e.g., cants or wedges) should be inside the boot if possible (see Chapter 6).

Check stand-up skiers for leg-length difference. If found, make the necessary equipment modifications with straight lifts inside the boots or on the ski and then determine if additional canting is warranted. Last but not least, check whether the student needs heel or toe risers or fore/aft adjustment of the binding. All changes to a skier's stance should be made in small increments and periodically evaluated for function and comfort.

When considering equipment options and adjustments, the assessment at the start of the lesson will help narrow your focus. Understanding the student's disability, motivations, attitude, and cognitive abilities will help you select appro-

priate gear and make helpful modifications. Although too many equipment variables exist to cover them all, the following scenarios serve to illustrate the likely equipment choices indicated by a given student assessment.

SCENARIO #1

Trevor is a 42-year-old man whose left leg has been amputated 4 inches below the knee. He walks with a prosthesis, is self-conscious about his disability, and is afraid that he might get hurt.

Appropriate approach: Trevor should ski with outriggers, initially set tall to help him with his balance while sliding.

SCENARIO #2

Erika is 15 years old and has spina bifida. She walks with AFO braces and plays softball and soccer. Erika is strong and can stay active all day, but she sometimes has trouble with balance. Erika has weakness in her abductor, adductor, and gluteal muscles. Because she is paralyzed at the ankle, she has no sensation in her feet.

Teaching tactic: Erika should be able to ski with outriggers and a ski bra. Because of muscle weakness in her hips, she will probably need to use a closed stance or a spacer bar between her feet. This should be determined by assessing her functional stance. Erika may also exhibit extra pressure on her heels and might benefit from having her bindings moved forward to help apply pressure along the entire length of the ski.

Jasmine is a 36-year-old woman who has arthritis and has had multiple sclerosis for four years. She walks with braces, can stay active for up to two hours, and has weakness on her right side. Jasmine is on antidepressants and wants to ski to help her "enjoy life more."

Teaching tactic: Jasmine can ski with outriggers, but special consideration should be given to fatigue levels, high altitude, and stress. Skiing shorter runs with frequent chairlift rides provide rest breaks. The skiing portion of her lesson should last a half-day or less and should focus on having fun.

Stella is 45 and, due to polio, leans heavily on crutches and has a swing-through gait. She uses full leg braces and has a strong upper body.

Teaching tactic: Stella should be able to ski on a mono-board or on two skis attached at the tips with a ski bra and at the heels or mid-ski with a bungee cord. A slant board may be used to raise Stella's toes and help bring her to a neutral position. If lifts are used on the skis or in the boots, use a similar device to raise the outriggers. Use a parallel teaching progression.

Kendrick, 42, walks with a scissors crouch gait due to spastic cerebral palsy. He uses crutches, although not excessively and walks with his weight back due to weak quadriceps.

Teaching tactic: Place heel lifts in Kendrick's boots or have him use a slant board with the heels raised. This will help bring him forward to a neutral stance. He may also need

a ski bra attached to the ski tips, and perhaps a spacer bar for the heels. Non-corrective canting (i.e., to fill space without changing the natural stance) is appropriate. To provide stability and make it possible to ski on a flat ski, place padding inside the boot on the outside (lateral) half of Kendrick's foot.

Teaching Information
BEGINNER/NOVICE ZONE

As shown by the scenarios above, you have many equipment options available when teaching four-track skiing. You also have several choices when it comes to selecting an appropriate teaching progression. The following information describes teaching progressions appropriate for the four-track skier: (1) wedge progression, (2) parallel progression, and (3) walker progression.

Although these progressions have differences based on the abilities of the skier, they also have many similarities and begin with similar exercise aimed at teaching the basics of good skiing.

Introducing the Equipment

Before going onto the snow, take time to explain equipment function, setup, and proper use. If the student will be using outriggers, demonstrate how they work in the up (crutch) and down (skiing) positions and explain how they can be used to control speed. The student should become familiar with the equipment and practice using the outriggers in various positions.

If the student will be using a walker or ski-legs, select the appropriate fit and describe its use. The height and width of the equipment should be adjusted to support the skier in an efficient stance. Appropriate hand holds or forearm cradles should be present to help the student maintain stability.

Demonstrate how the equipment works in relation to the skis and skier. Explain how you can use reins to help the student control speed and turn shape and reassure the student that you will always be in control of the walker. Instructors should understand that walker-type devices have on-hill limitations and must be used with the utmost care and safety awareness.

Before selecting equipment, the instructor should have determined the student's need for tip or heel stabilizers, lifts, and cants. Do not use heel stabilizers without a tip stabilizer.

Flatland Drills

- Develop comfort moving on the flats with the aid of outriggers or a walker.
- If outriggers are used, experiment with outrigger placement and both the crutch and ski positions.
- Practice getting in and out of bindings.
- Engage in a game of "follow-the-leader" to gain experience moving around on the flats and shuffling along with outriggers or the walker.
- Work on lifting one ski at a time while balancing.
- If needed, provide assistance in getting moving. Attach reins to the ski bra. You can move the student across the flats by working from in front. Use a steady pulling motion, rather than jerking the reins, to help maintain balance.
- Practice exaggerated movements up and down, side to side, and fore and aft to help expand range-of-motion and improve stance.

Because flatland work is often difficult and fatiguing for this type of skiing, your best option is to move the student onto the hill as quickly as safety allows. Using gravity requires less effort, and you can use reins or a two-point hold for speed control, turning, and stopping.

If balancing on the snow is difficult, check to ensure that the outriggers are providing enough vertical support, the ski bra and spacer bar are providing appropriate lateral stability, and the student has sufficient strength and coordination to maintain balance.

Sliding and Gliding, Straight Run

- Ski a straight run on shallow terrain with a terrain-assisted stop. Encourage standing in tall, comfortable position with eyes and hands forward.
- To develop a balanced stance, alternate between a high and low position, flexing and extending or moving the body fore and aft while sliding.
- If balance is fair while using outriggers, lift one outrigger, then the other.
- If a ski bra is being used, you may need to use a two-point hold or reins to help with movement on the flatter areas.
- Be prepared to provide assistance for students using a walker. Use reins attached to the ski bra or place instructors on both sides of the walker for stability and safety. Another instructor or volunteer can ski in an inverted wedge in front to provide a visual target, give verbal instructions, and help stop, if needed.

As part of the flatland and gliding exercises, make sure the student feels comfortable with controlling speed. Teach how to control speed using the wedge or outriggers.

Because fatigue can be an issue, have a chair or bench nearby during the lesson. A portable canvas and aluminum camp stool is a good option.

If the skis are not tracking straight, check for an unbalanced stance or improper equipment set-up. Make sure any leg length difference and need for canting have been addressed.

Students skiing with a walker should stay centered on the walker for best balance. Be sure the walker height, width, and ski length promote balance and stability while sliding.

Wedge, Parallel, and Walker Progressions

The primary differences between the following progressions are based on skiing ability.

The **wedge progression** is taught to skiers with independent leg movement. This type of student can stand in a wedge position and may have the muscular strength and flexibility to rotate the legs and move them laterally. Some students may prefer the wedge because of the natural positioning of their legs or the added stability of the wider platform. Examples of a student who might use a wedge progression is a below-the-knee amputee or a person with multiple sclerosis.

The **parallel progression** is used for students who are unable to hold their legs in a wedge. They may be able to stand for long periods but be unable to rotate their legs or move them laterally. Examples of a student who might use a parallel progression include a person who has had polio or someone who has arthrogryposis (fixed joints) or spina bifida.

The **walker progression** is used for students who require the added stability in order to stand while skiing.

First Turns: Wedge, Parallel, and Walker Progressions

- Practice making slight directional changes from the fall line and linking directional changes before graduating to whole turns.
- Point the nose and toes in the direction of the turn. Perform "look-at-me" exercises. While you ski backwards in front and turn, the student follows your movements and rotates the body in the direction of each turn.
- Encourage lower body movements, starting at the feet and moving up. Give directions such as, "Point your toes (or kneecaps) at me," or "Swivel your hips toward me," or "Stand harder on your left ski while you shine the headlights on your knees to the right."
- When outriggers are being used, turn both outriggers gently in the direction of the turn. This will help direct the upper body toward the turn and assist in turn initiation. See Chapter 5 for additional information on using the outriggers to aid turning.
- When a walker is being used, start in the fall line, look in the desired direction of travel, and steer the walker in that direction. The instructor should always keep a grip on the walker or use a retention tether for safety.
- If additional assistance is required, use hands-on techniques using a bamboo pole, two-point hold, etc., to encourage kinesthetic awareness.
- If all else fails, students should rotate their shoulders toward the turn.

In attempting to turn, some people occasionally lean too much in the direction of the turn, resulting in edge-lock. Select terrain that enhances learning, i.e., avoid too much pitch. Reinforce correct outrigger or walker positioning and a centered, flat-ski stance.

Some find it difficult to keep the outriggers or walker properly positioned on the snow. If these devices get too far in front, out to the side, or behind, the student will probably bend at the waist and have difficulty maintaining a tall, efficient stance. If so, recheck the equipment and make sure that its length is conducive to a tall, comfortable stance. You might also practice stationary exercises, keeping the outriggers or walker in the proper position.

If the lower body cannot be used to initiate turns, introduce proper outrigger use to compensate (see Chapter 5 for additional details).

Linked Turns: Wedge, Parallel, and Walker Progressions

- Start with small turns and increase the turn radius and arc.
- Encourage application of more pressure to the outside ski while turning.
- Make sure your student feels comfortable turning across the fall line and can control speed with turn shape. Then, gain mileage on varied terrain.
- Use the outriggers to assist in turning (see Chapter 5).
- For students who use a walker, try different tip stabilizer arrangements to enhance skill development as balance and strength improve.
- Use two ski bras, one on each walker ski tip (or walker stabilizer bar, if applicable) to secure it to the student's corresponding ski tip.

- Use two bungee bras in the configuration described above.
- Use one ski bra to attach the student's skis.
- Use one bungee bra to attach the student's skis.
- Walk, slide, or turn on the flats first, then on the slopes without any tip stabilizers.
- Move on to four-track skiing when the skier has the appropriate balance, strength, and motor control.

Be prepared to provide hands-on assistance when a walker is being used and bear in mind the significant limitations in terms of the terrain that can be skied safely and comfortably. Know your ski area's recommendation for appropriate terrain for the walker ski.

For students who use outriggers, turns will take longer to develop due to the absence of a strong rotary force in the feet and legs. The rotary force will instead be coming from a variety of locations (outriggers, hips, and shoulders). These skiers will benefit from strong outrigger movements and other rotary forces such as hip, shoulder, and whole body rotation.

If the student cannot tip the skis onto an edge via ankle, knee, hip, or spine angulation, banking is acceptable if within the student's abilities.

Riding the Chairlift

Show how to ride the chairlift safely and how to position the outriggers for loading and riding. Maneuver through the lift line and get into loading position with the outriggers in the crutch position. Prepare to load the chair with outriggers in the ski position. The student should sit when the chair touches the back of the legs and, after loading, raise the outriggers off the snow and slide back into the chair.

Have the student prepare for unloading by sitting upright with the outrigger shafts (still in the ski position) parallel to the unloading ramp. Outriggers in the crutch position can catch on the snow and cause a fall. When the skis contact the ramp, the student should stand up with a gentle forward lean, place the outriggers on the snow, and ski off.

If the student is able to stand and move somewhat without the walker, consider having another instructor carry it while you help the student on and off the lift.

Moving Toward Parallel Turns, Wedge and Parallel Progression

- Practice garlands in one direction, then the other.
- Practice extension movements in the direction of the turn at turn initiation.
- Practice edge-release movements with the inside ski.
- To enhance skidding, practice a traversing sideslip in which the student engages and releases the edges.
- On gentle terrain, show how to ski an uphill christie fan progression. Start by moving across the fall line and gradually progress into the fall line. Eventually cross the fall line in a full turn.
- Use the outriggers to aid turning (see Chapter 5).
- If extra help is needed, use hip or shoulder rotation to aid turning.

If students have trouble extending toward the turn, practice extending the ankle, knee, hip, and spine statically while standing still. Then practice garland turns, focusing on extension before moving into a full turn.

Some disabilities may make it difficult to match the movement of the right and left skis. Allow ample time for this skill to develop through practice. Continue to practice edge-release movements, while stationary and then while skiing.

Many four-track skiers must use upper body rotation to make the skis turn. Continue practicing proper outrigger use to reduce this need, which will allow the student to stay in a more appropriate position to begin the next turn.

INTERMEDIATE ZONE
Parallel Turns

- Focus on releasing both edges by extending the ankles, knees, hips, spine, and outriggers in the direction of the turn, thus moving the center of mass in that direction.
- Practice performing hockey stops on your command.
- Progressively shorten the turn radius from short to swing, then lengthen the turn radius.

- Sideslip down the hill in a corridor.
- Use the outriggers to assist in turning (see Chapter 5).
- If traditional methods are not effective, practice using different parts of the body to initiate the turn, such as hip projection and shoulder rotation.

If you observe over-rotation and over-skidding at the end of the turn, re-emphasize the importance of pressure and edging movements. Continue to help develop a more countered position to reduce over-rotation. You may also encourage earlier turn initiation, including use of the outrigger, to reduce over-rotation.

Students in this zone often have trouble reaching down the hill and moving the whole body in the direction of the new turn. Have them experiment with the varying amounts of extension needed to release the edges. Continue practicing a traversing sideslip or garland turns with just enough extension to release the edges, then flex to re-engage the edges.

ADVANCED ZONE

As four-track students move into the advanced zone, they tend to rely less on the outriggers for turn initiation and support. However, the outriggers can still be used effectively to facilitate short-radius and rotary-dominant turns and provide occasional aid in balancing. Review proper outrigger use for advanced skiers described in Chapter 5. You will also find many useful exercises and suggestions in the *Alpine Technical Manual* that can be easily adapted for advanced four-track skiers.

Equipment for Sit-skiers

chapter 9

This chapter discusses specifics for assessing and teaching students who ski while sitting, including both mono-skiers and bi-skiers. Refer to Chapters 10 and 11 for more details.

Assessment Specific to Sit-skiers

When working with obvious or potential sit-skiers, the initial student assessment (Chapter 2) should be supplemented by observing the following:

- For students who walk—and some sit-skiers do—are they using a cane, crutches, or a walker? These individuals may have the balance and stamina to stand or walk but may be unable to ski standing up or may choose sit-skiing to reduce the risk of injury. For example, someone with one leg (a potential three-tracker) may choose to sit-ski for fear of injuring the one leg.
- For students who use a wheelchair, what type is it? The type of wheelchair and add-on accessories can tell you about a student's balance and coordination and give insight as to which muscle groups have paresis. An electric wheelchair may mark a severe disability or non-athletic individual, while a wheelchair with a low seatback and no brakes generally indicates some ability to use torso musculature to balance. The rule of thumb is that individuals who are unable to push themselves in a wheelchair are not good mono-ski candidates but are suited to a bi-ski.
- Does the wheelchair have a seat belt, supportive hardware, armrests, a wheelie bar, or head rest? These items are signs that the student may not be able to attain an athletic position, indicating that a bi-ski would be appropriate.

SUGGESTED ASSESSMENT QUESTIONS

In addition to these observations, ask some or all of the following questions to gather additional information:

- Is the injury complete or incomplete? Incomplete nerve severance in the spinal cord may allow the student to have some feeling or muscle use below the level of injury. For instance, some people with spinal cord injuries in the cervical (neck) region can still walk. Generally, students with spinal cord injuries at or above the fifth thoracic (chest-level) vertebra (T5) are good candidates for bi-skiing.
- What level of feeling does the student have? Although paralysis below the level of spinal cord injury may be complete, sensory nerves may still function. If a student cannot use the legs but has feeling in them, find out what kind of feeling, i.e., is the student able to sense pressure, heat and cold, pain, etc?
- Does the student have sore spots on any part of the body? Pressure sores can be dangerous if not properly padded and treated and may actually trigger autonomic dysreflexia if they become severe. People with spinal cord injuries are more apt to get pressure sores because they do not feel when the skin is being pinched or rubbed by clothing or other objects. It is a good idea for both mono-skiers and bi-skiers to loosen all straps and readjust the equipment every half hour to allow blood to circulate more freely and avoid prolonged pressure or friction of any area.

SUGGESTED ASSESSMENT EXERCISES

A student's range of function can be assessed further using simple exercises to determine fore-aft and lateral balance as well as flexibility and strength. Try some of the following:

- Assess lateral balance by asking the student to lean to the left and then to the right while seated with arms extended.

- Assess forward stability by having the student lean forward while seated, and with hands placed on the abdomen.
- Assess flexibility and range of motion by asking the student to reach to the left and then to the right to pick up an object placed on the floor.
- Assess grip strength by shaking hands with the student.
- Assess shoulder and arm strength as well as stability and balance by pushing up, down, forward, and then back on the student's extended arms while he or she tries to resist.

OTHER IMPORTANT FACTORS

Other questions in assessing a student's potential for mono- or bi-skiing are whether the student has ever had any of the following conditions:

- **Frostbite**—If so, be aware that it tends to recur more easily in the same spot. You need to keep a vigilant eye out for signs of its return.
- **Broken bones**—Some types of disabilities result in weak or brittle bones. Extra precaution must be taken to prevent hard crashes.
- **Autonomic dysreflexia**—If so, the student is subject to recurrence of this life-threatening condition. Fortunately, students who have experienced it are more likely to recognize its signs and know how to care for themselves should it occur on the hill. Talk about it with the student and be clear on what the student expects of you if it occurs.

Equipment Selection

The choice of a mono-ski or bi-ski is determined by the student's physical abilities and attitude toward the sport. It is possible for people with functionally high spinal cord injuries to mono-ski, but the higher the injury level (i.e., the more of the body has paralysis or paresis), the more challenging and frustrating it can be to balance and control the ski. Bi-skiing provides a way to get started quickly for students who do not plan to ski often and just want to have fun, while mono-skiing may be the goal of more aggressive or athletic skiers. Remember, the ultimate responsibility for safety and equipment choice lies with the instructor.

Four types of sit-down equipment available are the sit-ski (like a sled with metal runners and a slippery plastic bottom), the mono-ski (one ski on the bottom) the bi-ski (two skis on the bottom), and the dual ski (a hybrid of the last two, using two skis). All of these are generic terms used to describe categories of sit-down equipment. The mono-ski is the most challenging piece of sit down equipment to use because it requires the greatest balance, strength, and coordination.

Mono-skis and bi-skis share a variety of components. For example:

- The **seat** may be made of fiberglass, orthopedic foam, plastic, metal, or any combination of materials. The purpose of the seat is to affix the skier to the ski(s) snugly so that any movements the skier makes will be transmitted through the seat to the ski(s). The seat should hold the skier in a dynamic position that allows effective use of musculature. This may include a variety of straps and padding for a tight fit. Still, the seat needs to be comfortable and not cause contusions or abrasions. The seat is equivalent to a stand-up skier's boot.

- The **frame** is the chassis or skeleton of the equipment onto which the other parts attach. It is commonly made of metals that are strong, rigid, and light weight. At least one company has a carbon fiber frame under development.

- The **foot tray** most commonly an attachment made of metal, plastic, or fiberglass. Its function is to provide a platform for securing and protecting the feet and lower legs, which typically attach to the foot tray with straps. A good foot tray should be adjustable for a range of skiers.

- The **suspension** consists of a spring or a shock absorber and serves a dual purpose: (1) it reduces the amount of jarring on uneven terrain, and (2) it keeps the ski(s) in contact with the snow for maximum control. Some suspension systems have adjustable spring tension and adjustable compression and dampening.

- The **linkage** connects the seat to the ski(s) and usually consists of moving swing arms that allow the suspension to work but restrict movement in other planes. This causes any rotary or edging movement by the skier to be transmitted directly to the ski(s). The type of linkage determines movement of the skier's center of mass fore and aft relative to the ski upon compression and extension of the suspension.

- The **binding** connects the linkage to the ski(s). Many bindings allow adjustments fore and aft relative to the ski without redrilling. Some bindings allow the ski(s) to flex between the front and rear of the binding for uniform decambering. Bindings without this feature create a flat spot in the center of the ski(s) that disturbs the arc in the snow.

- The **lift-loading** mechanism is a system of levers and swing arms that mechanically raises the mono-ski or bi-ski into position for loading onto a chairlift. A good lift-loading mechanism should be operable by the skier to allow as much independence as possible. Mono-skis or bi-skis without this mechanism generally requires the skier to ask for assistance in loading.

- Two types of **outriggers** are currently available: (1) hand-held outriggers, and (2) fixed outriggers. Here, the mono-ski and bi-ski differ, as fixed outriggers can be attached to the bi-ski for lateral support. Fixed outriggers are particularly helpful for skiers who have problems maintaining stability. Fixed outriggers can be used exclusively or in conjunction with handheld outriggers, but they significantly limit the terrain a bi-ski can negotiate. For example, the decreased lateral range of movement and limited edging produce long-radius turns that can rapidly cause the skier to accelerate, especially on steeper terrain. Accordingly, the use of fixed outriggers requires the use of a tether line controlled by the instructor or ski buddy.

- The **evacuation system** is some form of mono-ski or bi-ski to be evacuated from a chairlift using standard ski patrol techniques in the event of a breakdown (see photo 9.1). The evacuation system varies from a system of straps and carabiners to a rigid metal eyelet that the ski patrol can clip into. All mono-skis used on chairlifts should have some form of evacuation system. A good evacuation system should be able to lower an unconscious skier in the upright position during evacuation.

PHOTO 9.1 Lift Evacuation of a Sit-skier

Brian W. Robb

- The **retention strap** consists of a strong piece of webbing, usually attached to the back of the seat with a non-locking carabiner on the other end. Once on the chairlift, the strap is looped around the chairlift and clipped back to itself. Its purpose is to keep the skier from exiting the chairlift prematurely. Many adaptive programs and ski areas recommend retention straps. Note that the strap should be wrapped around the chairlift in a manner that takes out almost all of the slack to avoid becoming caught on the chairlift equipment and dragged around the bull wheel.

Mono-skis typically use a standard alpine ski, but just about any type of ski has probably been tried. Durability is an essential feature. Shaped skis work exceptionally well for mono-skiing. Many mono-skis are built on a "boot" (a sole piece made of metal or fiberglass) that can be snapped into a standard alpine ski binding. However, when using a standard binding, the binding should be "pinned" to prevent it from releasing.

Four types of skis are commonly used as bi-skis. The original bi-skis came with "Swingbo" (134 cm long and typically white) or "Alpin Surf" skis (typically 125 cm long and blue). These skis are relatively short and wide and feature asymmetrical side-cuts that are deeper on the outside edges. To promote flat-ski tracking and inhibit undesired skidding, the Swingbo or Alpin Surf skis have skegs (i.e., fins) on the running surface. "Challenge" skis, which began to appear on bi-skis in the mid 1990s, are approximately 132 cm long, yellow, and also feature an asymmetrical sidecut. However, Challenge skis generally do not have skegs, and articulation is stiffer than either the Swingbo and Alpin Surf skis. Stand-up "performance carver" or "super shaped" skis in the 140 to 170 cm range are the fourth common option for the bi-skier. These may be beneficial for the advanced bi-skier and require more rotary movements to effect a turn than the other, more radically shaped skis.

The bi-ski may have a "handlebar" or "control bar" attachment for the skier to grasp. The skis and seat of the bi-ski are linked through an articulating mechanism that allows the skier to simultaneously flatten the skis or tilt them onto corresponding edges. Pads or bladders dampen the articulating movements and help the skier return to a neutral position.

Bi-skis may also be equipped with a tether, which is generally not recommended for mono-skis. Attached to the back of the bi-ski, the tether allows the instructor to help the student control direction and speed.

Equipment Setup

Finding the optimal equipment setup for a student takes experience and a good deal of patience. Even the most experienced instructors may spend the better part of the first lesson fine tuning all of the adjustments to customize the equipment for the individual student. It is important for the instructor to write down what equipment was used and make note of to record the modifications to expedite the setup for the student's next lesson.

Fitting the equipment includes most or all of the following steps.

Ski Selection

Selecting the appropriate ski is important, although bi-skiers have few options. Select skis that attach properly to the equipment. Mono-skis have more options. A sturdy ski with some shape is recommended. Length is usually 140 to 170 cm for children and 160 to 200 cm for adults. Remember to tune the ski; a poorly tuned ski can be difficult to turn. Beginner/novice skiers generally find skis that are torsionally soft and flex easily to be more forgiving and easier to ski. Experts may prefer stiffer, more lively, less forgiving skis for better edge hold and more pop out of the turns. Beginners and freeriders (mono-skiers enjoying steeps, bumps, powder, parks, and halfpipes) will benefit from a 1° to 3° base bevel for easier edge release. Expert racers may want a 0° base bevel and aggressive side edge bevels (e.g., 3°) for better edge hold on firm snow.

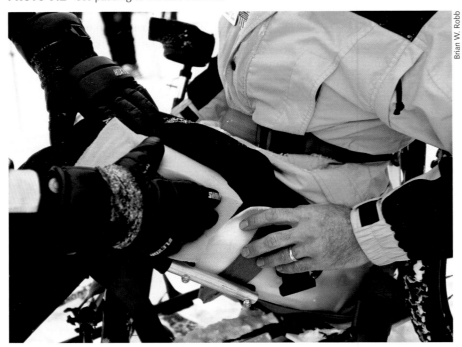

PHOTO 9.2 Use padding to increase comfort.

Seat, Straps, and Foot Tray

- The fit of the skier into the seat should be as snug as possible without sacrificing comfort. This means selecting or adjusting the seat to correspond to hip width. Auxiliary padding may be necessary to achieve a tight yet comfortable fit. Padding is especially important around the hips and thighs to keep the hips from shifting within the seat, as shown in photo 9.2.

- Straps can augment the fit and enable efficient transfer of the student's movements to a mono-ski. Additional straps may be needed to secure the hips. Avoid placing straps over a collection bag or catheterization tube. Restricting excretion is the leading cause of autonomic dysreflexia in disabled skiers.

- The height of the seat back is critical! Be sure to select equipment that has correct height or can be adjusted to fit the student. It should be high enough to support the highest muscle group

with paresis. In other words, the skier should have reasonably good control of all muscle groups that extend above the top of the seat back. However, be careful not to raise the seat back too much. If too high, the seat back will limit range of motion and impair balance, rotation, angulation, and pressuring of the ski. If the seat back cannot be adjusted high enough, add-on accessories can effectively raise the level of support.

  ▶ Kidney belts, back support belts, and inner tubes can provide additional support while allowing a degree of flexibility.

  ▶ Plastic back plates can be bolted on to effectively raise the height of the seat back.

  ▶ More advanced or committed students may want to have a special seat orthotically molded and customized to fit the specific disability and individual body shape.

- The foot tray should be adjusted to allow good contact between the thighs and seat bottom. In an ideal situation, the foot tray produces about a 90° bend in the skier's knees. This bend serves a number of purposes, including:
  - improving circulation and reducing spasticity in the legs,
  - stretching the muscles through the gluteus and lower back, which may assist in returning to an upright position from a forward flex, and
  - compressing the skier's mass about the axis of rotation, which reduces the moment of inertia and makes turning easier.

Dowel Testing

"Dowel test" the student by placing a wooden dowel under the ski (as described later in this chapter) so that the center of mass is over the "sweet spot" of the ski. The sweet spot varies depending on the kind of turns a skier intends to perform—from the mid-cord for rotated, skidded turns to about 4 to 5 inches back of the manufacturer's recommended center mark for carving. Freeriders and beginners tend to ski better when balanced on the mid-cord of the ski because the swing weight is minimized, allowing stronger rotary movements. Find the mid-cord of the ski by measuring its length from tip to tail and marking the center. Carvers and racers tend to prefer to be doweled over the manufacturer's center mark, which is usually well behind the mid-cord of the ski. Every major manufacturer marks the point on the ski where the center of the boot should be placed when mounting the skis for stand-up skiers. The mark usually represents the center of sidecut of the ski (i.e., the narrowest part of the waist of the ski).

Stand-up skiers are able to shift weight fore and aft considerably to work the entire length of the ski, but a mono-skier or bi-skier is limited in fore-aft movement. It therefore is vital to center equipment on the ski in a way that allows student to apply pressure to the tip or tail of the ski by leaning slightly forward or backward. While in the athletic position, a sit-skier should be perfectly balanced over the sweet spot of the ski.

A step-by-step description of dowel testing follows:

- Depending on the specific needs of the student (see above), find and mark "ski center" on the ski. This may be the mid-cord, the manufacturer's recommended center mark, or a spot between depending on the type of turn desired.
- Have the skier transfer into the ski, dressed in full ski clothes.
- Place a dowel under the bottom of the ski at the ski center and perpendicular to the ski.
- The student then takes the outriggers and assumes an athletic position.
- Assist the student in sliding forward or backward on the dowel until centrally balanced over it. This will be accomplished when the weight is equally distributed from tip to tail. The student should be able to pressure the tip of the ski with a slight head tip forward and pressure the tail with a slight tip backward. In extreme cases, you may have to actually add weight to the foot tray or seat back to get the student's weight centered over the dowel.
- Mark this centered position on the equipment frame. This could be termed the "frame center" mark.
- Make adjustments so that the "ski center" mark on the ski and the "frame center" mark on the equipment frame match. This final adjustment can be done with the skier in or out of the equipment.

Canting

The skier should be canted correctly to maintain lateral balance. Mono-skiers or bi-skiers commonly have a unilateral (in one direction) weight distribution, which tends to keep the ski(s) on edge instead of a flat bottom. An edged ski is hard to steer! This problem can usually be detected visually by the instructor. Place the student in the equipment on a hard, flat floor and see if the student can lift the outriggers into the air and balance. This maneuver should be easy, and the student should look symmetrical when balanced. If one shoulder is higher than the other, cant under one of the student's buttocks to achieve a more symmetrical position.

Another technique is to place the student in the equipment on a mat of dense foam (the kind that leaves an impression after you push your finger into it). The student then balances while lifting the outriggers into the air. Carefully lift the skier and equipment off the foam and notice the impression in the mat. The impression will clearly indicate which edge is bearing more weight. Place padding under the side with the deeper impression to tilt the student slightly toward the other direction. Repeat and adjust until both impressions are equal.

Canting can also be accomplished by inserting a thin wedge between the binding and the ski. Some mono-skis have an adjustment that allows the seat to be offset to one or the other side to achieve a flat ski.

Sit-ski Adjustments

- Adjust the outriggers (see Chapter 5).
- Adjust the suspension. Spring tension will affect handling and comfort. The rule of thumb is that a heavier skier needs greater suspension tension, while a lighter skier needs less. If the student is bottoming out, increase the tension. If the student is unable to compress the suspension, decrease the tension. Generally, tension should be set lighter for beginner/novice skiers, who usually generate less force, and heavier for more advanced skiers, who generate greater force through higher speeds and tighter turns.

Some high-end suspensions have controls for compression and rebound dampening. Compression dampening controls the speed at which a shock absorber can be compressed to help minimize bottoming out. Rebound dampening controls the speed at which a shock absorber extends after being compressed. Properly adjusted rebound dampening can help prevent skiers from being sprung into the air and losing snow-to-ski contact that is essential for good control. Check the manufacturer's recommendations.

Additional Measurements and Adjustments to Consider

MEASUREMENT OF LEFT AND RIGHT ANGULATION

- **Step 1**—With the skier fully strapped into the mono-ski and a full-length ski attached, position the ski on a piece of thick-pile carpet or foam to allow the skier to rock back and forth and side to side.
- **Step 2**—If you have an inclinometer, position it across the ski, as close as possible to its mounting point. Have the student angulate (i.e., lean to the side) as far as possible in one direction. The outriggers should be barely touching the snow and the student leaning over the ski to keep from falling. Measure the maximum angulation angle that can be reached in each direction.
- **Step 3**—If the amount of angulation in each direction is equal, no further adjustments are necessary. If the student can angulate farther in one direction that the other, the ski can be canted. For example, if the skier can angulate 10° in one direction and 6° in the other, a 2° cant will result in angulation of 8° in each direction. Although canting is best done on the ski, canting of the seat at the mounting point also works. In a program ski (i.e., a ski with a variety of users or a rental), stiff foam can be inserted into one side of the seat shell to shift the skier to the side.

MEASUREMENT OF ROTATION

Not all students can rotate equally. Some will be able to turn their upper bodies farther in one direction, which can limit their ability to make equal turns in both directions.

- **Step 1**—Ask the student to rotate as far as possible in each direction, noting the angle of trunk rotation at the shoulders. This can be done by sighting over the shoulders or extending a stick over the shoulders (taping it to the shirt) and having someone read the amount of rotation by looking down from above the student's head.
- **Step 2**—If the amount of rotation is equal in both directions, no further adjustments are necessary. If the student can rotate farther in one direction than the other, the seat can be rotated to compensate. For example, if the student can rotate 20° to the left and 10° to the right, a 5° seat rotation will allow a 15° rotation in both directions.

CONCLUSION

The information in this chapter is intended to assist the instructor in assessing students who will mono-ski or bi-ski. It also should aid in selecting equipment for the student and adjusting it for an enjoyable, safe, and effective learning experience.

Mono-skiing

chapter 10

In the adaptive world, "mono-skiing" has a very different meaning from the able-bodied ski technique with the same name. People commonly use the word "mono-ski" to describe a wide ski with two forward-facing bindings mounted side by side. In the adaptive world, a mono-ski is a piece of sit-down equipment that enables people with disabilities to ski sitting down.

Assessment Specific to Mono-skiers

Each mono-ski lesson starts with an in-depth assessment of the student, including his or her physical and mental condition and attitude toward learning to ski. The assessment should use a variety of methods to assess balance, strength, and range of motion.

A thorough assessment gives the instructor the information needed for selecting and adjusting the equipment to meet each student's specific situation. Refer to Chapter 9 for more detailed information on assessing the student and setting up the equipment.

Beginner/Novice Zone

At the start of the lesson, take time to introduce the equipment to your student. Consider explaining and demonstrating the following:

- Functional aspects of the mono-ski and its safety features.
- How the seat and straps allow a snug, supportive, yet comfortable fit.
- The purpose and function of the suspension.
- The lift-loading mechanism.

- The purpose of the retention strap.
- Use of the lift evacuation system.
- Use of outriggers. (Show how to change them from the crutch position to the ski position and back. Explain the outrigger brake.)
- How to transfer into the mono-ski.

FLATLAND DRILLS

After the student has become familiar with the equipment, go to a flat, uncrowded area with good snow cover. Based on your student's needs and abilities, help the student do the following:

- Push backward by engaging the outrigger claws. Use this opportunity to adjust the claws and contact bolt, if needed.
- Learn practical methods for balancing and moving around on flat snow.
- Put the outriggers in the ski and crutch positions.
- Push forward and backward with the outriggers in both ski and crutch positions.
- Lean fore-aft and side to side with the outriggers in both ski and crutch positions.
- Balance with outriggers off the snow.

PHOTO 10.1 Mono-skiing can be as dynamic as any other snowsport.

Brian W. Robb

- Perform a star turn by lifting and turning the whole mono-ski with outriggers in the crutch position.
- Put the ski into the "chairlift position" using the lift-loading mechanism and then maneuvering the ski.

At some point during the flatland drills, the student will probably fall. Take this opportunity to teach the student how to get back up. Take time to practice falling and getting up. Explain the importance of not trying to break a fall but instead focusing on keeping the outriggers from getting behind or beneath the student during a fall. Practice getting up with and without assistance.

To assist a mono-skier after a fall, place the mono-ski across the fall line with the outriggers uphill or across the lap. Stand with your uphill ski or boot against the mono-ski, then grasp the mono-ski from the highest point possible and pull it toward you, using your entire body. Be cautious to not put yourself, especially your back, in an awkward position. Use a one, two, three count so the student can help.

To get up unassisted, have the student orient the mono-ski across the fall line. Assuming the mono-skier is lying on the left side, both outriggers should be placed in the crutch position. The student then lets go of the left outrigger, letting it dangle off the wrist, and places the left palm or fist against the snow and uses the right outrigger (also on the left side of the mono-ski) to push up into an upright position (photo 10.2). To complete the move, the student might have to grasp the left outrigger while being supported by the right outrigger.

PHOTO 10.2 Using Outriggers to Get Upright From a Fall

Deacon Chapin Photography

SLIDING AND GLIDING, STRAIGHT RUN

When the student begins to feel comfortable with the ski, it is time to begin sliding. Try the following:
- Push students up the hill or have them propel themselves with their outriggers, depending on their attitude, strength, and disability.
- Turn students into the fall line or have them turn themselves using a star turn (see photo 10.3).
- Demonstrate and an athletic position, dynamic balance, proper positioning of the outrigger, and the importance of keeping the head up.
- Let students experience the feeling of sliding on snow on a gentle incline.
- Have them close their eyes while gliding in a straight run to "feel" the balance.
- Have them briefly lift both outriggers while in a straight run.
- Have them apply equal and progressively stronger pressure to both outriggers by flexing forward at the hips and spine, dropping

the elbows, and driving both hands down and forward to engage the outrigger claws and control speed.
- When the inevitable fall occurs, use it as an opportunity to practice getting back up unassisted.

If your area lacks gentle terrain or the student is timid, ski backwards in a reverse wedge in front during the straight run. This allows you to maintain eye contact with students, read their facial expressions, talk face to face in a reassuring manner, provide a feeling of safety, and stop them at any time.

Another technique for slopes that are steeper than ideal is to practice straight runs traversing across the slope. However, stay in a position to stop students that may start heading downslope.

Make sure students keep both outriggers on the snow at all times and with equal pressure. Look for level knees, hips, and shoulders. Tell students to keep their heads up

PHOTO 10.3 Orient the student into the fall line.

Deacon Chapin Photography

and look in the direction they want to go. For students that drive a car, use the following analogy: "When driving a car, have you ever noticed how hard it is to stay in your lane while looking at the road directly in front of you? It is much easier when you look farther ahead because seeing the visual horizon helps with balance."

At this stage, pay close attention to the movement of the outriggers. If they bounce roughly and lose contact with the snow, the brake needs to be adjusted (lessened). If the student's elbows are locked with arms extended straight out in front when attempting to brake, the outriggers are either too short or do not have enough brake. Check to see that both outrigger brakes are adjusted equally, and remind the student to brake equally with both arms.

Make sure students can feel the highest strap securing them to the mono-ski. Maintaining balance requires that mono-skiers are able to feel and control the muscle

groups below the highest strap. If not properly secured, the mono-skier's balance will be significantly compromised.

Mono-skiing requires precise body movements to control edge angle. If the student is not supported high enough, precise movements will be difficult. You may need to add a high-back, kidney belt, or some additional hardware to help the student feel and control the ski.

FIRST TURNS

When the student knows how to control speed with the outriggers, introduce direction changes. Refer to Chapter 5 for additional information on proper outrigger use.

Ski backwards in an inverted wedge in front of the student. Tell the student to follow you and concentrate on controlled braking to match your speed. Remind the student to look at you as you make a gradual turn. Most of the time, merely focusing on you is

enough to make the mono-ski turn in your tracks without the student making a conscious to do so. Practice this in both directions.

When the student can comfortably change direction by following you, introduce turning both outriggers with the hands to complete the turn. Remind the student to look in the direction of the turn. This should allow the skier to turn across the fall line and come to a stop. Practice making turns to a stop in each direction. Emphasize that turning across the hill and controlling turn shape are the primary methods of controlling speed for all good skiers and snowboarders. Encourage students to keep both outriggers on the snow to maintain a balanced stance.

In the exercises above, rotary movements of the head, shoulders, and outriggers to make the ski turn are introduced subtly. To accomplish these movements, the student must maintain a relaxed, centered stance to help keep a flat ski through most of the turn. Near the finish of the turn, the ski edges slightly as it comes across the fall line. The steeper the hill, the greater the edge engagement will be.

During these initial turning exercises, encourage students to maintain equal pressure on both outriggers. However, as they look in the direction of the turn, a slight lateral weight shift occurs, placing slightly more pressure on the inside outrigger. This subtle weight shift is considered a form of passive cross-over. Looking toward the turn directs the head (which weighs 5 to 7 pounds) across the ski. Make sure that students do not overdo these movements to avoid becoming over-edged and inhibiting the turn.

For students who have difficulty turning, check that they are maintaining a flat ski and following your movement with their head and shoulders. On flat terrain, have students pivot to the left and right to see if either edge is catching in the snow. If one edge consistently catches, adjust the sitting position to achieve a flat ski stance (see Chapter 9).

Moving a skier's mass forward on the ski will enhance turn initiation. A ski that is pressured at the tip will tend to seek the fall line as edging is minimized during turn initiation. For more on this subject, see "The Gravity Friction Principle" in George Twardoken's book *Universal Ski Techniques*, pages 86–88, (University of Nevada 1992).

Being able to turn in only one direction may indicate arm dominance and can be resolved with additional practice and time. For example, a right-handed person generally turns better to the right. Different brake settings on the two outriggers can also cause this, as can loose straps and canting problems.

CHAIRLIFT PROCEDURES

At most ski areas, students are ready to ride the chairlift when they can control speed using the outriggers and can turn to stop. Please follow the recommendations of your area in deciding when your students should ride the lift.

Ideally, find a three- or four-seat chairlift that services green terrain and has a safety bar. Teach the student how to safely use the chairlift with the help of one or more trained instructors. Here are some general steps that can help ensure safe loading of the mono-ski:

- Put the mono-ski into the load position.

- Practice loading outside the lift line on a stationary chair or bench before attempting to load the chairlift. During the practice load, each person involved (the mono-skier and one or two lifters) should be told exactly to do. Before loading, be clear as to:
  - who will communicate with the lift operators,
  - who will push the mono-skier out into the loading area,
  - where each person will grip the mono-ski,
  - what the load count will be and who is going to do the count,
  - how much each person will lift the mono-ski,
  - who will put the safety bar down,
  - who will be responsible for attaching the retention strap to the chair, and
  - who will make sure the lift operator is next to the safety switch.
- Communicate with the lift operator, using the hand signals that operators use to supplement verbal commands.
- Use the safety bar, if the chairlift is equipped with one and if it is compatible with your student's equipment.
- Loop the retention strap around the chair, taking out most of the slack and clipping it back onto itself.
- Review unloading procedures with the student once on the chairlift. Keep in mind that mono-skiers generally unload the chairlift at full speed, as forward momentum helps create smooth unloading.
- When students are ready, help them develop skills for self-loading the chairlift. Have them practice putting the mono-ski into the load position and propelling themselves through lift line. Have students who will

require assistance getting on the chairlift practice helping you by placing the outriggers on the snow in the crutch and pushing against them.
- Have the student practice counting the load, such as "one, two, three, lift!" Remember to use the retention strap and remove it at the top of the chairlift. You may want to ask the student to remind you about this important step.
- Have the student practice counting the unload, such as "one. two, three, Go!"
- The student practices unloading by throwing the outriggers and torso forward at the unloading ramp.

Many ski areas and adaptive teaching programs require that sit-down skiers request a slow chair before boarding the lift. It may be easier to board the chairlift if the lift operator is requested not to hold or "bump" the chair, which can throw off the timing of the load. Ask the lift operator to eliminate the side-to-side swing as the chair comes around the bull wheel.

LINKING TURNS

Once students can turn to a stop, it is time to begin linking turns. Turns can be linked by steering both outriggers in the direction of the turn. See Chapter 5 for more details on using the outriggers at this stage.

You might also want the student to practice traversing. Make sure to point out that the mono-ski's edge is slightly engaged in a traverse. The amount of edge is a function of the slope angle. Use the following analogy: "Skiing is simply a matter of letting go of the hill, turning the ski, and then grabbing back onto the hill. To let go of the hill, you need to take your ski off edge (flatten the ski) by leaning slightly down the hill. To turn the ski, look where you want it to go and move the outriggers in that direction. To grab back onto the hill, just sit centered and balanced in a traverse."

Try any of the following exercises based on the needs of your student.

- Use garlands to work on turn initiation and finish.
- Take off your skis, get down on your hands and knees, and show the student, using one ski as a prop, that an edged ski does not want to rotate on the snow and a flat ski does want to rotate.
- Have the student practice following your track in the snow as you lead down the hill (after putting your skis back on), picking a line that establishes speed control through turn shape while avoiding obstacles. Constantly remind the student to "feel for" a flat ski.
- Try to encourage your student to "look at you" with the upper body, and not just the head, to encourage some countering. The upper body should remain stable, quiet, and remain pointing slightly more down the fall line than the lower body and ski.

Movement of the head, shoulders and torso in the direction of the turn, in combination with turning the outriggers toward the turn, creates enough force on the ski to turn it effectively and efficiently. Turning the torso creates stored rotary energy in the body (like a twisted rubber band). When the energy is released by flattening the ski, the upper and lower body will realign. This energy helps to guide the lower body and ski into the new turn.

Movements at this stage should emphasize passive edge engagement in a traverse, flattening the ski to

PHOTO 10.4 Performing a Seat Assist

Deacon Chapin Photography

turn, and a gentle re-engagement of the edge at the finish of the turn. The ski flattens due to a subtle weight shift, either active or passive, as the mono-skier goes down the hill. Looking with the head and body toward the new turn distributes slightly more weight toward the inside outrigger, creating a stronger rotary effect through increased friction.

If the terrain is too steep or the student is unable or unwilling to commit to the fall line a "seat assist" may be a useful teaching tool (particularly for kinesthetic learners—those who learn by feeling). A seat assist (photo 10.4) is a hands-on approach in which the instructor straddles the mono-ski from behind and holds the seat to guide it.

Remind the student that both outriggers should be touching the snow at all times to allow instantaneous balance corrections by shifting pressure from one to the other. If outriggers are held off the snow, they must first be placed on the snow before they can be pressured differentially, greatly increasing reaction time.

PHOTO 10.5 Carving with a mono-ski is an exhilarating experience.

Brian W. Robb

Students sometimes have trouble transitioning from one turn to the next. The student may be leaning back or into the hill. This impedes turn initiation, and a flat ski will seek the fall line only if it is not pressured behind center.

Although leaning uphill is human nature, students must overcome this instinct. One method is to keep students at very slow speeds and encourage them to shift their weight onto the downhill side of the buttocks when starting a turn.

Some skiers, typically those who have ridden motorcycles or bicycles, rely on ski design to turn rather than keeping a flat ski and skidding. Their reflexes have been trained to lean into turns, and riding the edge feels natural to them. As shown in photo 10.5, carving is an exhilarating experience. However, it should be saved until a skier is comfortable controlling speed and changing direction.

Intermediate Zone
ENHANCING CROSS-OVER

As students move into the intermediate zone, helping them make an effective cross-over movement of the center of mass is critical. Focus on proper turn initiation in which the upper body and both outriggers are moving in the direction of the new turn. Refer to Chapter 5 for more information on outrigger use at this stage. Try some of the following, depending each student's specific needs.

- Ski garlands, focusing on individual components of turn initiation or turn completion.
- Have the student practice following your track in the snow.
- Apply light pressure or reach with the outside outrigger to begin forming angles in the hips and spine.
- Test how high an edge angle the student can achieve while sitting statically.
- Check how quickly and accurately the student can turn every time you yell out "turn."
- Practice slipping into the fall line from a static position with skis across the fall line.
- Modulate hip and spinal angulation to go from an edged traverse to a slipping traverse and back.
- From a static position across the fall line, see how far the student can reach down the hill without falling.
- While initiating a turn, see how far down the fall line the student can reach the outrigger without falling.
- Practice high-speed hockey stops on your command.
- Make smooth short-radius turns, then make short swing turns with a more abrupt edge set.
- Practice a falling leaf.
- Have the student practice self-loading the chairlift with you in a hands-on position in case a loading error should occur.

Balance is maintained through constant contact of the outriggers with the snow. As speeds become greater and turn radius shorter, forces affecting the mono-skier become greater. To balance against these greater forces, the student begins to incline toward the inside of the turn. The student should maintain contact with the outside outrigger to reduce banking.

As the mono-skier begins a turn, the head, shoulders, arms, and outriggers should move toward the center of the turn. This flattens the ski and shifts pressure toward the inside outrigger, allowing the skier to create a rotary force as the outriggers are steered in the desired direction. The combination of these movements is referred to as "committing to the turn."

One of the most difficult parts of learning to mono-ski is overcoming the fear of committing to a turn. The steeper the terrain, the more commitment is required to flatten the ski. Here is a simple exercise that works wonders for teaching a student to commit:

- Stop with the ski across the hill (perpendicular to the fall line) on beginner terrain.
- Point the downhill outrigger directly down the fall line so that the downhill arm and outrigger are creating a 90° angle to the mono-ski.
- Drop the elbow to engage the outrigger brake.
- Look down the hill and lean forward.
- If the weight is transferred to the downhill outrigger (i.e., the upper body and hips shift slightly down the hill), the tip of the mono-ski will slip into the fall line. When it does, allow the student to complete the turn and try it again on the other side.

- Make sure the student starts from a complete stop, and do not allow "paddling" around the turn with the uphill outrigger. After the student has successfully mastered this exercise, encourage feeling the same body position and making the same commitment to the downhill outrigger while skiing.

As students begin to commit to the turn, be cautious of edge-lock caused by making the cross-over move before creating rotary movements. If a mono-skier moves aggressively in the direction of the turn without creating any friction with the inside outrigger, the ski will not have enough force to come around and will get stuck on the inside edge—probably leading to a fall.

Advanced Zone

A mono-skier at this level is in the process of learning how to ski any run in any snow condition and is able to ride any lift alone. The mono-skier is learning to refine movements such as carving, hip check and hip projection, and mastering everything the mountain has to offer, including competitive skiing. Try any or all of these exercises with your student and refer to Chapter 5 for additional insights on proper outrigger use.

- Ski the bumps.
- Ski the powder.
- Ski the crud.
- Ski the steeps.
- Train on a race course.
- If the student has usable musculature in the lower torso, try hip check turns and hip projection turns.
- Stand at the bottom of the hill and have the student watch you for turn commands. Move your poles from side to side in a slow, rhythmic fashion like a metronome.

Each time you move your poles, the student turns in that direction. This exercise develops rhythm and flow.

- Ski in an inverted wedge down a steep hill while your student remains within the corridor defined by your ski tips as you plow snow. Tell the student to focus on you and direct the inside outrigger straight down the hill toward you at turn initiation.
- Do synchronized turns with your student.
- Practice self arrests on steep terrain.
- Practice slide recoveries on steep terrain. After a fall, the student presses against the hill and slides on the side of the seat bucket. This position allows the friction of the outrigger to be used as brakes while the mono-ski is turned downhill and across the fall line. While still sliding, the student pushes off the hill with the uphill hand, reaches the downhill outrigger to meet the snow, and tilts the pelvis to get the ski's edge to engage. If done correctly, the student will pop upright and can continue skiing.

Be forewarned, however, that a student who is not prepared to resist the forces generated by this maneuver could end up in a downhill edge-catch slammer.

At this stage, students learn to use appropriate tactics for any given terrain. They can move aggressively into the turn. This aggressive cross-over move puts the ski on an early edge, enabling a carved turn. The outriggers should have minimal brake to reduce rotary movements or skidding.

To set up correct hip and spinal angulation for carving, students must keep their shoulders parallel to the terrain. In other words, if you were to balance a yardstick across a student's shoulders it would always be parallel to the snow beneath the skier at any given time. With the skier positioned across the fall line during the initiation of a turn, the downhill shoulder would be lower than the uphill shoulder in an amount proportional to the steepness of the hill. The steeper the hill, the greater the difference in the height of the shoulders. As the skier proceeds into the turn, the shoulders begin to level out until the skier is directly in the fall line. At the fall line, the shoulders should be the same height and perfectly level. From the fall line to the turn finish across the hill, the inside shoulder continues upward and the outside shoulder downward until the skier is back to the starting position, with the downhill shoulder down and uphill shoulder up.

Even the most expert mono-skiers occasionally have trouble loading and unloading chairlifts. Especially when the mono-skier is loading an unfamiliar lift, it is a good idea for you to keep your hands on the mono-ski to deal with any problems that may arise. Some combinations of chairlifts and mono-skis are incompatible. For example the chairlift may be higher than the mono-ski's loading height. Remember, ski areas are worried about uphill capacity and safety. If you are unsure about a mono-skier's ability to safely ride a chairlift, keep your hands on the mono-ski. This will help the loading to go smoothly and keep the lift from stopping.

Bi-skiing

chapter 11

Bi-skiing is an adaptive downhill ski technique in which the skier is seated in a device attached to an articulating undercarriage mounted on two uniquely designed skis. The design of the bi-ski (see photo 11.1) and the abilities of the student and instructor enable a person with a high level of disability to ski at most areas.

The bi-ski fills a niche created when mono-skis joined sit-skis as an option for individuals who cannot, or choose not to, ski standing up. Since the advent of the bi-ski, a fourth option, the dual or twin ski, has also been developed. The dual/twin ski is a hybrid apparatus that is more stable than a mono-ski and allows easier independent loading on a chairlift than a bi-ski. However, the bi-ski is the most stable apparatus for sit-skiing.

Since its inception, the bi-ski has been viewed by some instructors as a second-place alternative to the mono-ski. This is an unfair characterization. The bi-ski is not a lesser piece of equipment and, when used to its potential, can enable a skier to master black diamond terrain and experience the wonders of the entire mountain.

Assessment Specific to Bi-skiers

The skier assessment information for mono-skiers described in Chapter 10 is applicable for bi-skiers. A critical part of the assessment is for the instructor to get a good understanding of the student's goals. For example, a goal of skiing with friends or family on intermediate terrain one weekend a year would indicate different equipment than a goal of skiing independently off piste several times a season.

The following scenarios profile hypothetical bi-skiers and how to assess their abilities based on their control of torso musculature.

SCENARIO #1

Hunter is a 30-year-old C4 quadriplegic who does not have the ability to grasp any sort of device (outriggers or handlebars) and whose sitting balance is derived from the support of the bucket and associated straps. He is able to tilt his head from side to side, thus creating a minimal amount of a cross-over movement.

PHOTO 11.1 Bi-ski

Brian W. Robb

Teaching tactic: Hunter's bi-ski setup will be with or without fixed outriggers, depending on the instructor's preference. The instructor may elect to use a hands-on steering assist ("bucket assist") that does not require fixed outriggers. However, because a bucket assist requires that the instructor remain in contact with the bi-ski, emergency stops are very difficult. The instructor may wish to use short tethers with fixed outriggers and encourage Hunter to assist with the edge cross-over by tilting his head in the direction of the intended edging movement. To assist with his sitting balance, chest and shoulder straps will be used and adjusted for a snug fit.

SCENARIO #2

Skye is an 8-year-old student with athetoid cerebral palsy affecting all four limbs. She cannot grasp or control handheld outriggers, but with a grasping aid may be able to hold onto a handlebar or similar device affixed to the bi-ski. Skye is able to move her center of mass by shifting her head and arms from side to side. Without the use of the fixed outriggers, she has virtually no ability to balance in an upright position.

Teaching tactic: Skye will use a bi-ski configured with fixed outriggers and without hand-held outriggers. The instructor should explore free-form lateral movements of Skye's head and shoulders. If appropriate, Skye should be encouraged to move her arms laterally to help make a cross-over movement. If possible, both arms may be moved to the same side of the bi-ski for stronger cross-over.

A control bar may be used if uncontrollable spastic movements cause an oscillation of the bi-ski due to rebound of the fixed outriggers off

the snow. Skye's hands are secured to the handlebars with Velcro™ gloves or duct tape. Sitting balance may be assisted with chest straps securely adjusted but without shoulder straps to allow more freedom to push away from the handlebars and initiate a cross-over motion. When fixed outriggers are used, the bi-ski must be tethered.

SCENARIO #3

Jason is an 18-year-old student with C6 quadriplegia who cannot grasp or control hand-held outriggers but who is able to shrug his shoulders enough to move his arms from one side of the body to the other. His range of lateral and fore-aft movement is extremely limited and must be supported with chest straps.

Teaching tactic: Jason will ski in a bi-ski configured with fixed outriggers and without hand-held outriggers or a handlebar. Tipping his head and shoulders while pulling his arms across his lap in the direction of the desired cross-over will effect an independent edge change. Chest and shoulder straps will be needed, although shoulder straps should not be over-tightened to avoid impeding cross-over movements. Since Jason will use fixed outriggers, tethers are required.

SCENARIO #4

Carron is a 40-year-old woman with multiple sclerosis who can grasp outriggers but, due to muscular or neurological deficiency, must use some type of aid to hold the outrigger. She cannot grasp the cords to flip the outrigger tip up or down. Her range of lateral and fore-aft motion is minimal unless initiated by arm and outrigger use. Arm strength and coordination is impaired to the extent that Carron may have difficulty supporting her weight at a 45° angle or returning to a neutral, balanced stance from that angled position.

Teaching tactic: Carron will ski in a bi-ski using hand-held and fixed outriggers and will need to be tethered. She will need Velcro™ gloves or duct tape to help affix the hand-held outriggers. She may need a loose-fitting chest strap but probably not shoulder straps. Carron will initiate cross-over by pushing off with her uphill outrigger and moving her center of mass down the hill in a banked body position. As the bi-ski changes edges, she will block her upper body with the new inside outrigger and allow her hip to drop into the new turn, causing an angulated edging movement. As Carron progresses and her balance increases, she may be able to remove the fixed outriggers. It is possible that she can eventually use rotary movements initiated by the outriggers to assist the turn.

SCENARIO #5

Hannah is a 30-year-old student who skied one weekend a year with her family before her injury five years ago. She has T12 paraplegia and has the strength and ability to firmly grasp outriggers and can resist when you attempt to pull them out of her hands. She can grasp the cords and flip the outrigger tip into the up or down position. She demonstrates good range of lateral and fore-aft motion using her torso musculature. Hannah can maintain good balance and, when leaning on the outriggers to the right and left (about 45°), has the strength to extend her arms and return to a centered position. She is able to angulate at her hip and spine while keeping her head upright and shoulders level, and she can shift her center of mass voluntarily and without difficulty. Her goal is to be able to ski again with her family on their annual vacations.

Teaching tactic: Hannah will ski in a bi-ski using hand-held outriggers without fixed outriggers. She will use all waist, leg, and foot straps but will not need any chest or shoulder straps. Hannah will initiate cross-over by pushing off with her uphill outrigger and moving her center of mass down the hill. As the bi-ski changes edges, she will block her upper body with the new inside outrigger and drive her hip and lower torso into the new turn, causing an angulated edging movement. As Hannah progresses to an intermediate skier, she will learn to initiate rotary movements with her outriggers by using a cross-over movement similar to that used by mono- and dual-skiers.

Teaching Information

The following progressions summarize teaching a skier how to bi-ski, from beginner/novice through advanced phases of skiing. Separate progressions are outlined for teaching bi-skiers using hand-held and fixed outriggers.

Unlike any of the other adaptive techniques, the primary movement used to turn in bi-skiing is edging, not rotation. Thus learning to control a skid is introduced much later in a bi-skier's progression than in other disciplines. Other differences are also noted in the summary.

Instruction on how to safely load and unload a chairlift is as important for bi-skiing as the other adaptive disciplines. A typical bi-ski lesson will use two instructors for loading and unloading the chairlift. Loading and unloading are best learned in a practice setting. Each ski area and adaptive ski school may have its own policy regarding adaptive ski equipment on chairlifts. The instructor is responsible for knowing the specifics of these policies.

Bi-skiers using fixed outriggers follow a shorter progression than those using hand-held outriggers due to the assistance of tethering or hands-on assistance. A progression for teaching skiers using fixed outriggers is included at the end of this chapter.

BEGINNER/NOVICE ZONE
Introduction to Equipment
Before students transfer into the bi-ski, help them become familiar with the equipment by doing the following:
- Demonstrate how the seat and straps hold the skier in a snug, supportive manner.
- Explain how the articulating undercarriage enables the skier to turn.
- If hand-held outriggers are used, demonstrate how they function. Explain the brake claw and the cord used to flip the tip up or down.
- If fixed outriggers are used, explain how they augment balance.
- If a handlebar assembly is required, explain how the skier will hold and use it.
- Discuss tether lines and how they are used to assist the skier.
- Finally, demonstrate the function and use of any mechanical chair-lift loading features of the bi-ski and explain the use of the evacuation system.

Flatland Drills
- Achieve a functional, athletic stance, balanced, and sitting tall yet slightly flexed. Sitting balance is enhanced by the support of the seat and accompanying straps.
- Locate an outrigger position that offers the most lateral support. Have students briefly lift the outriggers off the snow to test balance. Have them balance using only one outrigger for support.

- Have students lean to the left and right, supporting their weight with the outriggers, and then return to a neutral position.
- Teach how to use the outriggers to push forward and backward. Typically, pushing backward will be easier.
- Flatten the skis and pivot them left and right, with or without an unweighting motion.
- Practice falling and getting up. Raise the outriggers out of the way before falling to the side. To get up unassisted, have students position the bi-ski across the fall line with the body uphill. Place the outriggers uphill and push with the edge or tail of the outrigger tip and rebalance.
- To help students get up with a full assist, position the bi-ski across the fall line, take hold of the bucket, place your foot/ski below the bi-ski, and bring it upward to an upright position.

For students who have difficulty balancing in the upright position, make sure the outriggers are sized appropriately and that the students know how to use them to aid balance. Outriggers that are too long force students to shrug their shoulders to accommodate the length or maintain excessive bend at the elbows. Shorten the outriggers so the arms are almost straight, with the shoulders relaxed and the outrigger tip close to the skier's hip.

If a student has difficulty maintaining a neutral position, check whether dampening devices are in place, that pads or cants have not shifted, and that all straps are in place and adjusted correctly.

Sliding and Gliding, Straight Run

- Push the student up a slight hill so you can steer the student into or slightly across the fall line. Stronger students can try pushing themselves up the hill with their outriggers.
- From a bullfighter stance (i.e., bracing against the outriggers and facing down the fall line), the student flips the outriggers down (into the skiing position) and glides down the slope to a terrain-assisted stop. Some students find it easier to leave the outriggers in the down or ski position and simply turn the outrigger inward, toward the bi-ski, to hold themselves with the edge of the outrigger tip. When the student is ready to glide, it is simply a matter of pointing the outriggers straight down the hill.
- Teach students how to control speed with the outriggers.

First Turns

- Experiment with varying the outrigger positions laterally and fore-aft to find the advantages or disadvantages of each, particularly concerning balance.
- Help students discover how varying the amount of lateral tipping of the bi-ski changes the radius and speed of the turn. Use static drills to help students feel the position needed to turn the ski.
- From a bullfighter stance in a traverse, students begin moving across the hill. Next, they tip the bi-ski downhill so the edges engage and the ski begins to turn. Have the students hold this position, passing across the fall line, until coming to a stop.

PHOTO 11.2 "Drop and Block" Technique

Brian W. Robb

- Experiment with adding angulation by lowering one hip. Explain that this takes some of the weight off the inside outrigger and shifts it over the support of the bi-ski seat without sacrificing edge angle. The inside outrigger may be used to "block" the upper body from leaning into the turn. This aids angulation at the hip (see photo 11.2).

Linking Turns

- Ski quick, angulated little turns (i.e., "wiggle turns") down the fall line of a shallow slope, maintaining square shoulders and an upright head while using angulation ("hip drop") to turn.
- At initiation of the turn, introduce a "push off" with the uphill outrigger to achieve cross-over to the new edges.
- Encourage use of turn shape rather than outrigger braking as the primary means of speed control.

- Drop the inside hip toward the snow to establish a kinesthetic awareness of good body position during angulated turns.
- Perform a series of garlands to become comfortable with turning into the fall line from a traverse and to reinforce the amount of edging movements required to maintain a traverse.
- After linking several turns, come to a stop by finishing a turn across the fall line using turn shape to stop and not relying on the outrigger brake.

The push off, block, and hip drop sequence creates angulated edging movements even in students who cannot control their torso and allows the center of mass to be supported by the muscles and skeleton of the upper body instead of the arms and outriggers. As students gain speed, they may need to move the outriggers forward 1 to 2 inches to help overcome the increased resistance of friction on the snow. If the student is physically unable to resist the increased outrigger friction, attach a bungee cord or surgical tubing between the outrigger shaft and the front of the bi-ski. The length of bungee or tubing must keep the outriggers close to the "power position" (i.e., next to the hips rather than close to the knees) without being pulled behind the bi-ski.

Riding the Chairlift

Students with a disability that makes them incapable of stopping or turning without instructor assistance also need an instructor for loading and unloading the chairlift. After a quick introduction to what to expect, they are ready to go. Other students need more training so that they can become progressively more independent. Begin by teaching them on a chairlift that services green terrain. When students are ready is based on the terrain available and your ski area's policy for riding a chairlift. Develop the student's ability to use a chairlift with the help of one or more instructors or, if appropriate, teach how to use a self-loading bi-ski. For example, you might try using this sequence:

- Explain entry into the lift line to the student and volunteer or other assisting ski instructor.
- Pick a route that is as safe and simple as possible.
- Try a practice load outside the lift line.
- Synchronize the lifting and loading commands between you, the student, and the assistant.
- Review hand signals for "Stop," "Slow down," and "Okay."
- For a two-person loading team, discuss where the second person will be positioned (i.e., riding the lift, standing beside the lift without skis, etc.).

Consider and plan ahead for the following:
- communication with the lift operator
- moving into the loading area
- chairlift speed for loading, riding, and unloading
- use of the safety bar and retention strap
- correct unloading procedures

Anticipate potential problems and have a plan for addressing or avoiding them. Let the operator know of any special needs regarding chair speed or if help is needed positioning the student. Ask the operator to be prepared to hit the stop button in case of a problem. In the event of a "misload" in which the bi-skier is thrown forward onto the snow, try to protect the skier's head as the chairlift passes over. Fixed outriggers on the bi-ski may catch on the chairlift. If this continues to be a problem, whether from ramp height or the chair cushion, a precautionary measure is to remove the fixed outriggers before loading the lift.

Adding Mileage with Linked Turns

- Explore varying turn shape and turn radius on comfortable terrain.
- Practice increase and decreasing the amount of angulation (hip drop) to "carve" the turns.
- On shallow terrain, do a series of brief direction changes ("wedge wiggles") to encourage early edge change and prevent overturning.
- The student follows your track as you ski in an inverted wedge in front.
- Show how to self-arrest after falling and sliding.
- Explore self-loading techniques.

INTERMEDIATE ZONE
Controlling Rotary Movements

- Introduce and encourage a controlled skid through increased speed, steeper terrain, and decreased turn radius.
- Teach use of a countering movement of the chest and shoulders to control skidding and reduce spinout, i.e., a skidded overturn.
- Teach how to control skidding between turns by turning the downhill outrigger in the direction of the new turn without moving the outrigger from the power position (outriggers remain near the student's hips).
- Explore different turn sizes and discuss the benefits of each on varying terrain.
- Lengthen the outriggers as the student progresses to steeper terrain.
- Negotiate a slalom course, improvised from ski poles or piles of snow, that requires a change in turn radius or rhythm.
- Encourage an intentional overturn, staying committed to the inside outrigger to reinforce safe correction of an overturn. The bi-ski is designed to carve a turn moving backward as well as forward, returning the skier to a proper orientation with the fall line.

To reduce over-turning, encourage moving the head, shoulders, outriggers, and as much of the torso as can be controlled in the direction of the new turn before the skidding starts. Double check that the student is balanced over the middle of the skis by observing the point where snow spray originates. Re-doweling of the sit-ski may be necessary as skills improve.

Enhancing Cross-over

- Encourage moving the outrigger away from the hips and forward to mid-shin (mono-ski style).
- Lengthen the outriggers so the student can touch the outrigger ski to the snow with the outrigger shaft approximately in line with the shins and a slight bend in the elbows.
- Reinforce extension movements in the direction of the new turn.
- Refine extension and flexion movements of the torso to correspond with the initiation and control phases of the turn.
- Develop short-radius turns.
- Reinforce the importance of combining angulation (hip drop) with the new rotary movements.
- Experiment with increased speed control by skidding at the end of the turn.
- Explore equipment options such as Challenger or "performance carver" type skis that do not have a skeg.
- Explore extension or "returning to neutral" movements to initiate a new turn and encourage flexion movements throughout the control phase of the turn.

If the student tends to oversteer some turns, encourage moving the outriggers toward the new turn earlier in the completion phase of the previous turn. Ensure that the student stays countered, which will help avoid excessive skidding.

As outriggers are moved forward and away from the power position, students need to adjust their balance over the support of the seat and skis and may not have sufficient arm and torso strength to support their weight. Therefore, introduce this movement gradually, based on the student's physical abilities and confidence.

ADVANCED ZONE

- Teach a more aggressive cross-over by extending the inside arm and torso in the direction of the next turn (down the fall line).
- Introduce increased countering movements of the head, shoulder, and torso earlier in the turn, coordinated with the downhill (inside) outrigger.
- Augment edging movements with "push-off, cross-over, and spine extension" movements of the uphill (outside) outrigger.
- Increase the effectiveness of rotary movements by shifting the outriggers farther away from the axis of rotation.
- Introduce bumps and off-piste skiing and explore terrain-assisted pressure control movements.
- Use falling leaf exercises to develop fore and aft pressuring, corresponding with tip and tail release.
- Try "target skiing" in which the student's head, shoulders, and torso point toward a downhill target throughout the turn.
- Practice short-radius turns for speed control on steeper terrain.
- If the chairlift seats are suitably low, teach strong, agile bi-skiers to self-load or provide enough loading impetus to eliminate the need for a second instructor.

If students have problems maintaining speed control on steeper terrain, continue to emphasize counter motion throughout the turn. Discuss the importance of outrigger placement for the intended turn and terrain. Similar to the location of the pole touch for a stand-up skier, the bi-skier's placement of the outrigger should be directed to the center of the new turn (i.e., long radius turns will require an outrigger placement

closer to the feet while short radius turns require a placement perpendicular to the hips).

TEACHING BI-SKIING USING FIXED OUTRIGGERS
Flatland Drills

- Have students try to balance over the skis using subtle movements of the body and arms, possibly in conjunction with a handlebar system.
- Show them the difference between balancing in the left-side, neutral, and right-side positions. Small, smooth movements separated by a pause will prevent oscillation or bouncing of the bi-ski.
- Focus on how movements of various parts of the body affect movement of the bi-ski. It could be as simple as a head tilt, shoulder drop, lateral movement of one or both arms, or a hip dip. With practice, students can develop the ability to isolate those movements.
- If a student is skiing without the handlebar and using the arms to initiate side-to-side movements, work on a smooth cross-over of the arms.

First Turns

- With assistance from you or a tetherer, have students begin to descend the fall line of a shallow slope. As speed increases, have students shift the center of mass moving the head, shoulders, or arms toward the desired turn (photo 11.3).
- If a handlebar system is used, encourage students to pull or push, as they are able, to lever the center of mass toward the desired turn.
- Have students perform a turn to a stop in each direction.

PHOTO 11.3 Gain momentum, then shift the center of mass toward the desired turn.

Bi-skiers using fixed outriggers may experience oscillations (wild, uncontrolled bouncing from side to side) from a combination of forces and rebound from the fixed outrigger. Ensure that the student remains close to the fall line and attempts to return to neutral between turns. The fixed outriggers should be adjusted to engage the snow early. Also, use sufficient dampening devices. With some types of disabilities (most commonly, spastic cerebral palsy), use of a control bar may reduce the movements that cause oscillation.

Linking Turns

- Have students initiate a turn, as discussed previously.
- Teach to cross the fall line and return to a neutral position, with or without assistance.
- Have students take a deep breath between turns to help find the center of mass.
- Teach to initiate a turn in the opposite direction, with or without assistance.
- Teach to maintain a consistent speed and avoid turning too far or slowing down too much.
- If needed, increase the use of the tether line to help students with turn initiation and speed control on steeper terrain. By positioning yourself appropriately, you can increase tether leverage without having to exert significant strength.

Fixed outriggers inherently restrict the turn radius of the bi-ski, thus limiting the terrain available for safe and controlled skiing. However, students with good upper body strength and balance may be able to ski some types of bi-skis on more difficult terrain with the use of hand-held outriggers (see the hand-held bi-ski progression discussed previously).

- If needed, assist a student's turn by using the tether line. As the student starts to initiate the turn, pull down on the downhill tether and lift up on the uphill tether. Imagine turning a very large steering wheel in the direction—one hand dropping down as the other lifts up.
- If needed, increase the tension on the tether line to help control speed.
- Cue students when to make turns to help maintain momentum. Without adequate momentum, the fixed outriggers tend to bite into the snow and could tip the bi-ski over.
- Perform garland exercises to help develop comfort with shifting the center of mass.
- Show how to complete a turn across the fall line to come to a stop.

When a student first starts moving in soft-snow conditions, it is very important that both outriggers are off the snow and the bi-ski is pointed slightly down the fall line. This is best accomplished with two instructors: one holding the tether and the other positioning the student. A bi-ski with fixed outriggers will not gain enough momentum when going from a standing start to a traverse to initiate turning (the bi-ski will tend to keep turning up the hill). Additionally, if the student begins with the downhill outrigger on the snow, this leads to awkward, unbalanced position.

Because the fixed outriggers inhibit carving, the skis may remain relatively flat on the snow, causing the student to drift into the fall line. This can be complicated by multiple fall lines. Anticipate and avoid such an occurrence by constantly analyzing the fall line of approaching terrain. If this is not possible, stop the bi-ski with the tether and help the student out of the troublesome area. You can also manually grasp the bi-ski, flatten the skis, and pivot the ski in a manner that redirects it.

Adaptive Snowboarding

chapter 12

Snowboarding is another fantastic activity that can be used to create positive experiences for people of varying ability levels. Snowboarding has a "cool" factor that is attractive to all ages and appeals to many disabled snowsports enthusiasts.

This chapter is not all-inclusive but instead is intended to help guide the adaptive instructor toward ideas for equipment selection and use and skill development. Thus, not every piece of adaptive snowboarding equipment is highlighted, nor is every scenario illustrated. Any instructor who is seriously teaching or guiding disabled riders should explore additional resources to develop further understanding of topics mentioned in this chapter.

PHOTO 12.1 Adaptive Snowboarding

Brian W. Robb

Safety

Safety of both the student and instructor are the top priority in any lesson. More than merely reflecting responsibility and common sense, creating a safe learning environment is key to a student's feeling of confidence and comfort. Students who feel unsafe are much less able to learn and enjoy their experience.

Assessment Specific to Adaptive Snowboarders

The following overview describes the more common disabilities likely to be encountered by instructors or guides of adaptive snowboarders. Through experience, adaptive instructors will gain experience with these and other types of disabilities—particularly as equipment and techniques continue to be developed, opening up this wonderful snowsport to a wider range of users.

Visually Impaired

Students range from having minor impairment in one eye to total blindness in both.

■ Consult Chapter 4 for a discussion of equipment orientation and guiding.
■ A conventional progression is recommended to build a full complement of skills for this student.

Hearing Impaired

Students range from having minor hearing loss to complete deafness.

■ Communication is a critical issue that needs to be addressed.
■ A conventional progression is recommended to build a full complement of skills for this student.
■ Coach toward visual and kinesthetic clues while riding.

Mentally Impaired

Students have disabilities related to brain functions including cognitive, memory, judgment, reasoning, emotions, and attention spans.

■ Consult Chapter 3 for more information about communication and teaching of the mentally impaired.
■ If the impairment does not affect the student's physical abilities, a conventional progression is recommended.
■ If the impairment does affect the student's physical abilities:
  ◗ assess the student's strengths and weaknesses,
  ◗ focus on what the student can do, and
  ◗ choose a path that best meets the student's goals, safely.

When selecting exercises, choose one the student can perform successfully. Build from small successes toward the goal.

Anatomically Impaired

Students have muscular, skeletal, or neurological impairments that affect strength, coordination, balance, and ability to voluntarily control movements.

- Assess the closest point of control to the board (e.g., shoulders, hips, knees, ankles).
- Based on the student's abilities, build a progression that allows the student to see improvement and realistic skill development quickly.
- Remember, there is no "right" way to stand on a snowboard. Stance should be based on what works and is comfortable, not how it looks.
- Choose balance aids with the intent to minimize their use.
- When dealing with prosthetics and knee braces, be aware of hinge mechanisms and braces. If the student's legs are fixed into a rigid position, he or she will make snowboarding movements from higher in the body.
- When riding a chairlift, the braces or prosthesis may need to be unlocked to allow a comfortable sitting position.
- To prevent the board from pulling too much on a prosthetis while riding a chairlift, an extra strap may be used to support the weight of the board.

When assessing students and creating a student profile, keep the following considerations in mind:

- Build a menu of the student's abilities and the factors that may affect these (i.e., medications, stamina, types of prosthesis, etc.).
- Assess the student's strengths, weaknesses, motivation, previous experience, etc.
- Identify the student's goals so the lesson can be focused accordingly.
- Based on the information gathered above, choose the appropriate equipment and teaching method that will maximize the student's experience and success.

Equipment Choices

This chapter assumes that the instructor or guide of an adaptive snowboarder is already an experienced rider and familiar with different types of snowboards (freestyle, freeriding, alpine/racing), boots (soft, soft step-in, hard), and bindings (strap or step-in). As a refresher, see the *Snowboard Technical Manual* (AASI 1998).

Selecting appropriate equipment begins with an assessment of the student's abilities and limitations:

- Check to see if students can flex their ankles, reach their feet, and tie their boot laces or buckle binding straps.
- Determine how close to the board they can make body movements (i.e., shoulders, hips, knees, ankles).

In general, a directional, longitudinally and torsionally soft board (e.g., a freeriding board) is the easiest to learn on. As the rider's skills and speed increase, the options will become broader.

PHOTO 12.2 Hard Boot Setup (Note: Rider is also using a leg-support device.)

Boot selection is critical. The boot must provide the appropriate amount of support—but how much is appropriate? A rider with minimal lower leg strength or lacking the ability to make fine ankle adjustments would benefit from a stiff boot—whether a soft or hard shell (photo 12.2). A rider with fine motor control in the lower extremities would benefit from boots with a sufficient range of flex to allow more precise control of the board with the feet.

After the boots have been selected, the interface or binding can be chosen. Plate bindings are generally very responsive and translate movements directly to the board—whether good or bad. The forgiveness is minimal. Step-in plate systems are available but require use of the upper body to release. The boot liners can be modified to fit different feet and the boot shell, being plastic, can be modified to a point. The shape of the shell dictates how the foot and lower leg will be held.

Step-in bindings with soft boots are widely available and offer several advantages. The effort to get in is minimal and can be accomplished standing up. Release again requires reaching down with a hand. Responsiveness is directly related to how snugly the boot fits and the amount of "play" between the boot and the binding. Adjustment of this boot/binding system is through use of liners, shims, and minor shell modifications.

Strap bindings are the easiest to adjust and customize and can be made to work with almost any boot. Responsiveness can be adjusted through strap tension, boot tightness, and the stiffness of the binding.

One last point to consider, as appropriate: soft boots are "cool." Hard boots and plate bindings are considered the realm of racers and "old" riders. While this is a relatively minor consideration to the end goal of turning someone on to snowboarding, it is important to consider your student's sense of self. Feeling cool and fitting in as much as possible with other riders on the mountain can be an important factor in confidence and a positive attitude.

Adaptive Tools

As with adaptive skiing, a wide variety of specialized equipment is available for adaptive snowboarding. Choosing from among these tools is dictated by a student's strengths and weaknesses. Keep in mind that these aids are merely to assist and not to be depended on. The goal should be to develop independence from accessory equipment through effective riding. Safety should always be of utmost concern whenever an aid is being used.

The following list of props and methods is by no means comprehensive but may provide a starting point to help you provide your students the best opportunity for learning and progressing.

Ski Poles

These tools can be used to aid balance while standing, walking, and climbing and can be tapped together to help visually impaired students. An instructor can assist alignment and turning by using poles to "connect" with the student—front hand to front hand and back hand to back hand. This method provides good control of speed, turn shape, timing, and moderate edging.

Outriggers

This versatile tool can be used to aid balance while standing, walking, and climbing by flipping the tip into the crutch mode, and while riding by flipping the tip into the ski mode. Use of one or two outriggers will depend on the needs of the student.

- Select or adjust outriggers so the student can stand comfortably upright with the outriggers resting gently on the snow. The rider should not rest on the outrigger while sliding.
- Use of two riggers or low (forward) stance angles can cause the upper body to be turned across the lower body, bringing them out of alignment. This typically causes the board to want to turn in the heelside direction. Forward angles are more conducive with two outriggers. When using outriggers of equal length, steering comes from the upper body. Because of the forward stance, this directs more pressure toward the front foot, creating a natural pivot point around which the board turns. Tilt of the board will be minimal as long as equal weight is placed on each outrigger. To create more edging, lift—or lighten—the downhill outrigger slightly. This generates edging through inclination as the center of mass moves toward and over the working edge. This can be effective at lower skill levels.
- It is possible to use a longer outrigger in the front hand, with the length set so that it can easily reach in front of the nose of the snowboard with plenty of clearance. Having the student direct the lead (longer) outrigger in the intended direction of travel helps move the center of mass over the working edge. This allows the rider to maintain a more neutral alignment. The back outrigger can be used to aid balance as needed. While turning, the back outrigger can be lightened (heel side) or lifted (toe side) to create edging through a blend of angulation and inclination. Turning (rotary) forces come by directing the upper body and hips toward the turn. More pressure is directed toward the lead foot with the goal of a pivot point between the feet.

Bamboo Pole

A bamboo pole can also aid balance while standing, walking, climbing, and riding. While sliding, the pole can be tipped to the inside of the turn and used to provide a focal point for the turn. However, encourage your students to not become dependent on the pole for balance while sliding. Turning the upper body toward the nose of the board while using a bamboo pole creates rotary input to the board. Pressure is directed toward the front foot, creating a pivot point under that foot. Edging is created through inclination as the rider tips to set the end of the pole inside the turn.

Horse and Buggy

This consists of a bicycle inner tube wrapped around the rider's hips and attached with carabiners to rigid (PVC) poles, tethers, or a hula-hoop. This allows the hips to be guided in the intended direction and can be used to control turn shape, speed, and timing.

HulaHoop™ or Wheelchair Push Rim

Use of a rigid hoop provides a way to connect the instructor and student without being hands-on.

- Holding the hoop face-to-face allows good communication between rider and instructor. This allows students to balance and create edging primarily on their own. Slight pressure shifts may be made, and strong upper body steering movements can be directed from the instructor. Timing of movements is key so that instructor movements do not adversely affect the rider's balance.
- When the student is placed inside the HulaHoop™, the instructor may move around the student while maintaining contact—but remembering not to upset the rider's balance. This method allows the instructor to effect rotary movements from the hips and upper body, slight edging movements from the hips, and minor pressure changes. The goal is for the student to maintain balance independent of the instructor.

Board Buddy

This piece of equipment (photo 12.3) is essentially a wind-surfing boom with a harness inside that attaches to the boom at four points.

PHOTO 12.3 Board Buddy Learning Tool

Brian W. Robb

The harness should be set at or slightly above the rider's hips. The rider then grasps the boom in front with the hands. The instructor can move around the boom to be face to face with the student or to guide from behind. The instructor can provide constant verbal encouragement and coaching while riding next to the student, but the student can not rely on the board buddy for support or to aid in balance. Rotary forces come from steering the rider's hips in the intended direction with the board buddy. Pressure may be directed lengthwise or across the board by moving the student in the desired direction. Edging can be created through direction of the hips over, or slightly inside, the working edge. Use of the board buddy does not restrict the rider's ability to twist the board with the feet.

Tethers

These consist of webbing straps attached to either the rider's hips or the board. Using either method, the student maintains balance and creates edging and pressure forces independent of the instructor, although the instructor can provide rotary input.

When tethered to the board, gentle adjustments and guidance are crucial to prevent strong reactive forms of balancing movements. Tethers may be attached to the nose and tail of the board using eye-bolts or to the rider's feet. Attaching tethers to the nose allows strong turning input (e.g., with a big student/small instructor), while attaching to the feet is more appropriate for a small student/big instructor. Experimentation will show what works best for you and your student.

Mono-board

This tool is a mono-ski bucket attached to a snowboard (see photo 12.4). Movement plans for this method can be adapted from those outlined in Chapter 10 (mono-skiing) and Chapter 5 (use of outriggers). Be aware of the wider platform of the snowboard and associated flat-tool pivoting skills.

PHOTO 12.4 Mono-board

Brian W. Robb

Mono-boarding differs from most snowboarding in the sense that the rider faces forward in the equipment instead of having a toeside/heelside orientation to the board.

Remember that use of adaptive equipment may affect the student's natural stability and balancing movements. Every effort should be made to gently direct the student's center of mass in the intended direction of travel. Sudden or strong input may cause resistance and ineffective movements. Mistakes or inconsistencies in your guiding may have a detrimental effect on the student's ability to maintain balance. As the instructor, it is your responsibility to be mentally and physically prepared ahead of time for the movements your are asking your student to make.

Teaching Concepts

The concepts set forth by AASI for student/teacher interaction are a solid foundation for any type of information sharing. Consult the *Core Concepts* manual and the AASI *Snowboard Manual* for more information regarding teaching concepts.

Sample Progressions

When developing a progression for students, remember the following elements:

- Ask what they want to do.
- Assess their current abilities.
- Understand what skills are necessary to achieve their goal.
- Mutually develop a series of small goals leading to the overall goal.
- Build up the skills needed to accomplish the goal using small, achievable steps.

AASI has developed a six-tiered structure to generalize student ability levels. The levels are designed as a basic assessment tool to help you evaluate students and their movement patterns and guide them to the appropriate classes.

Assess each student's closest point of control to the board and then determine which performance concept (PC)—twist, tilt, pivot, and pressure—will work best for that student. Although all of the PCs are important to successful riding, weakness in one may be offset by strengths in others. When building skills appropriate to the student's level, remember the student's ultimate goal.

Directional movements lead students toward the ability to manage speed through turn shape much earlier in their riding careers. Encourage students to stop by sliding across the hill rather than using a sideslip. A traverse is very effective and will lessen the potential for catching the downhill edge when changing edges.

At all levels, be careful not to move forward too quickly. A basic level of mastery should be evident before progressing to new terrain or a new skill. This is evidenced by students who do not need to look at their body to ensure that it is doing what the brain is asking. Movements may be somewhat stiff and mechanical but

are blended together without a distinct pause between. Students at this stage benefit more from adding mileage to anchor correct movements through guided practice rather than constantly adding something new.

The following is the breakdown of levels in the AASI *Snowboard Manual*:

- Level 1—New to snowboarding
- Level 2—Able to use lifts and ride the bunny hill
- Level 3—Able to make toe/heel side turns on green terrain
- Level 4—Comfortable riding blue terrain, some park and pipe
- Level 5—Comfortable riding black terrain and park and pipe, some off-piste
- Level 6—Able to handle anything the mountain can throw at them— all conditions, all terrain

LEVELS 1 TO 4, EARLY SKILL DEVELOPMENT

- Introduction to equipment, hands on
- Getting in and out of bindings

Mobility Exercises

With the board attached to one foot:

- Skate, using back foot, use props such as a HulaHoop™, push and glide (uses edging and pressure skills).
- Walk in big circle, wagon train, push and glide (uses edging, pressure, and steering skills).
- Pick up board, flick snow (uses pressure skill).
- Walk around it standing in one place, carousel, hop on back foot (uses edging and steering skills).

Straight Run to Direction Change, First Turns (Back Foot Out or In)

- Push and glide, back foot on, basketball stance, use aids, hand to hand (uses pressure (equal) and edging skills).

- With back foot out or in, tip board for slight direction change, up with toes (heel side), push front knee (toe side), front hand over toes/heels, slight lean in direction (uses edging and pressure skills).
- Full turn to gliding stop; back foot stays on (if loose), slows down as rider crosses hill at finish of turn, basketball stance, look where you want to go, balance over working edge, and patience turn.

Linking Turns, Both Feet In

- Traverse using front foot steering, balance on both feet, turn back uphill to slow down, looking where you want to go (uses edging, pressure, and rotary skills).
- Garlands, focusing on finish and start of turn, balance on both feet, front foot steering, turn back up hill slightly to slow, turn nose of board downhill to gain momentum (uses edging, pressure, and rotary skills).
- Link turns, maintaining momentum to help start of turn (i.e., not stopping between turns), focus on where you want to go, steering with front foot and knee in intended direction, maintain balance on both feet, finish turn by riding back across hill (traverse) to manage speed (uses edging, pressure, and rotary skills).
  - Add rhythm, counting, singing, follow me, stay in the track, do what I do (great for timing of movements).
  - Add flexion/extension, tall as a house/small as a mouse, count up/count down, rise to start turn, shrink to start turn (great for timing and helps to release old edge, increases balance over new edge).
  - Add flow, blend the two items above to help develop flow down the hill.

- Changing turn size
  - Rhythm and flow, count out for turn size, more numbers for longer turns, less for shorter turns, same count just quicker cadence, slow music for longer turns, fast music for shorter turns.
  - Flexion/extension, same movements but shorten time frame, same movements correspond to same parts of turn regardless of turn size.
  - Tactical approach, steeper terrain calls for short, round, skidded, finished turns; shallower terrain allows longer, rounded, more carved, finished turns or longer radius, unfinished turns to maintain/generate speed.

Elementary Park and Pipe

- Static hops and spins, spring from feet and ankles rather than hips and shoulders if possible, turn from head and shoulders, land in flexed stance to absorb, ollies and two-footed hops.
- Hops in traverse and in straight run, ollies and two-footed hops, develop ability to land without falling or lose edge, hop over little snowmen, bamboo, ski poles, build small ramp to help with timing of jump to clear object.
- Flat spins, board stays on snow, rider turns board all the way uphill, rides out switch, either on same edge (falling leaf) or change edge as board stalls (loop to loop style), smooth movements, upright stance, balanced on both feet, turning head to look where rider wants to go, start with 180s, build to 360s, one at a time to putting them together in a series.
- Switch riding, new front foot steers the board, balance on both feet, eyes looking where they want

to go, linked turns.
- Air 180s, from the toes, spin back foot around with toes leading and eyes looking toward landing (frontside), spin back foot around with heels leading and eyes looking back at takeoff (backside), land on toes, balance on both feet; ollie (rebound unweighting); two-footed jump (up unweighting); ride over bump (a type of terrain unweighting).

LEVELS 5 AND 6, ADVANCED SKILL DEVELOPMENT

Continued development and refinement of skills for advanced snowboarding are similar for adaptive and non-adaptive riders. The key, as with the other snowsport disciplines, is to rack up the miles and gain as much experience in as many different snow and terrain conditions as practicable. Improvements come from a combination of enhancement of motor skills and increased confidence in the ability to cope with new and changing conditions.

Conclusion

As the sport of snowboarding has increased in popularity, more and more people are becoming interested in learning how to ride, including students with disabilities. The information in this chapter will help you provide a safe, enjoyable, and rewarding snowboarding experience to the student. To increase your skills as an instructor and guide in assessing your students needs, helping them select appropriate equipment, and developing the most effective learning progressions, explore additional resources. Check *The Professional Skier*, *The Pro Rider*, and the PSIA and AASI websites for more information about adaptive snowboarding. Most important, be open to learning as you go and view all students as learning opportunities.

Adaptive Nordic Skiing

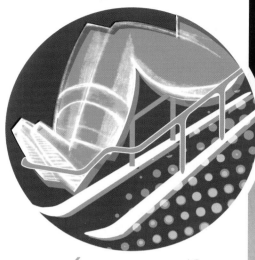

chapter 13

Nordic skiing is a wonderful option for people with disabilities who enjoy exploring nature trails, hiking, and being in the mountain environment. They come to the mountains to enjoy the quiet, soothing atmosphere, and their desires run the gamut from short, flat jaunts on a circular track to exploring backcountry trails.

As with other snowsports, the nordic teaching progression for skiers with disabilities has evolved as instructors and students explore different and innovative approaches. Being an adaptive instructor gives you the opportunity to share what you know about the sport and the mountain environment, learn about disabilities and the resiliency of the human spirit, and have more fun than you would have ever imagined. Watching students in any discipline attain their goals is always rewarding; in adaptive snowsports, the rewards are doubly so.

Nordic Stand-up Skiing

For stand-up nordic, the basic progression for classic (diagonal stride) and freestyle (skating) techniques includes:

- Balancing and maneuvering on skis
- Gliding on skis
- Moving from ski to ski
- Propulsion
- Poling and timing of movements
- Changing direction (including wedge, half wedge, and step turns)

Rather than describe these steps here, it is assumed that an adaptive nordic instructor is already well versed in teaching nordic techniques to stand-up skiers. The PSIA *Nordic Manual* (PSIA 1995) includes a detailed discussion of teaching nordic skiing. Other chapters in this manual provide information on how to assess the nature and extent of the disability and how to communicate, deal with problem behaviors, and incorporate specific teaching approaches.

Each of the six basic components of nordic skiing listed previously can be modified to meet the individual needs of adaptive students. The components can be adjusted—and some skipped entirely or only briefly touched on—because of pre-disability experience with the sport or transferable skills from other sports and life experiences.

PHOTO 13.1 Adaptive Nordic Skiing

Courtesy of Michael Byxbe

One issue that adaptive instructors commonly face is misalignment of the skis due to asymmetrical leg length or hip position or position of the feet relative to the legs or prosthesis device(s). A good rental repair shop can usually remedy the problem, and experienced instructors may be able to make these adaptive adjustments.

Otherwise, adaptive and non-adaptive stand-up nordic skiing are identical, except for specific aspects of the disability that require special communication or other teaching skills. To perform stand-up nordic, students must have two functioning lower appendages—whether their own feet and legs or prostheses—and in most cases two functioning upper appendages. Nordic skiing with one arm is possible and does not require specialized equipment or techniques (see photo 13.1). Nordic students with more severe disabilities, especially involving paraplegia or loss of one or both legs without prostheses, are directed to nordic sit-skiing as their passport to the backcountry snowsports experience.

Nordic Sit-Skiing

Use of a bi-ski for nordic is perhaps the newest of the adaptive disciplines and is a natural outgrowth of the evolution in equipment that was first applied in alpine sit-skiing. Nordic sit-skiers are basically the snow-sports equivalent of a wheelchair athlete—those committed and amazing athletes who compete in road races, wheelchair basketball, and wheelchair polo, among other sports. Because the discipline is new, it is in even more of a state of flux than the other adaptive snowsports; instructors interested in this discipline should make the effort to research refinements to equipment and teaching techniques regularly.

PHOTO 13.2 Nordic Sit-ski

Courtesy of Michael Byxbe

EQUIPMENT

Most adaptive nordic skiers use a sit-ski constructed of metallic tubing with hook-and-loop straps and an adjustable ski mounting system for various track widths. Frames are constructed in a variety of styles and often are custom built. For students with a more severe disability a pulk (a sled pulled by a guide) may be a more suitable alternative.

The sit-ski (photo 13.2) serves the function of a stand-up skier's boots and bindings by affixing the skier to the equipment in a way that transmits the skier's movements to the ski. The frame should hold the skier in a dynamic yet comfortable position that allows effective use of the musculature. Components of a sit-ski include the following:

Seat

The fit of the skier into the seat should be as snug and comfortable as possible. This means selecting a sit-ski so that the hip area corresponds to the skier's hip width. Padding may be necessary to enhance performance

and feel and prevent pressure sores. Straps augment the fit and enable efficient transfer of the skier's movements to the ski. Be sure that straps do not cross a collection bag or catheterization tube. The height of the seat back is important. The seat back should be high enough to support the highest muscle group that has paresis, but a seat back that is too high will limit range of motion and impair balance, rotary movements, and angulation. To brake and turn the sit-ski, the student must be able to touch the ground with both hands at the same time. A frame lower to the ground enhances control and performance and makes it easier to right the equipment after a fall.

The foot tray creates a 35° to 45° angle in the knees of the seated skier. The bend in the knees serves three purposes. First, it improves circulation and reduces spasticity in the legs. Second, it forces the hips back into the seat for a more secure fit. Third, it stretches the muscles of the gluteus and lower back, allowing the skier to return upright from a forward flexed position with greater ease.

Two types of seat are commonly used: molded or canvas. A molded seat is typically heavier than a canvas seat but keeps the student better connected to the equipment. A canvas seat needs more straps to secure the student. The flexibility of a canvas seat allows it to be used by a wider range of skiers, but eliminating excessive movement is almost impossible.

Bindings

Racers and serious recreational sit-skiers use the same kind of bindings (Profil, SNS, NNN, etc.) as stand-up cross-country skiers, except that two pairs are needed instead of one to secure the frame to the skis. Because of the quick release system, these bindings, while costly, are easier to store, transport, and wax, and they allow selection of different skis based on terrain, snow conditions, and type of activity planned on any given day.

Another alternative is to bolt the skis to the frame. This system is not quick release and frequently gets out of alignment, especially after a fall.

It is recommended that the student or volunteer carry a wrench in case adjustments are needed while on the trail. The bindings are mounted about dead center on the ski, or the front mounting shoe goes where the binding would normally be.

Skis

Ski length and type are a matter of personal choice. Use of waxless skis or waxing for grip is not necessary and creates more work in an already physically demanding sport by adding more friction to the system. Longer skis (185 to 200 cm) provide extended glide at the expense of maneuverability. Shorter skis are easier for beginner/novice students but do not hold well at high speeds. Some of the short skating skis may be too stiff to allow full contact with the snow, resulting in excessive sliding and reduced control. Softer skis are generally better for control and edging. When the student is seated, mid-section of the skis should sit flat on the ground. The skis are mounted to the frame about $7\frac{1}{4}$ inches apart (inside edge to inside edge) to fit the groomed track width.

Poles

Think of poles as extensions of the arms. Unlike alpine skiers, cross-country skiers need to use their arms and upper body for forward locomotion and braking. Appropriate pole length varies depending on terrain, ability of the skier, and personal preference. To measure for pole length, have the student sit in the frame with the tip of the pole on the ground. The top of the grip should reach between the chin and top of the head. Try different lengths to determine what size works best. Longer poles, while uncomfortable at first, provide better power,

especially going uphill. Shorter poles are generally easier for beginners and individuals with certain disabilities and allow for a faster "turnover" rate. Poles with skating baskets are necessary for groomed trails. The smaller triangular baskets allow the poles to plant with minimal resistance and maximal push.

Strength is an important consideration when choosing poles. Sit-skiers apply more force to poles than stand-up nordic skiers. Overly fragile "high-performance" poles, while reducing weight, may not hold up.

Finally, make sure the straps on the pole grips are adjusted correctly. Properly adjusted poles allow for a longer push stroke and longer rest time for the opposite hand and arm.

Outriggers

If a sit-skier is particularly unstable, fixed outriggers may be attached to the frame to improve balance by preventing a fall to one side, whether while stationary or in motion.

Tethering Devices

Cross-country skiing, especially in a sit-ski, is a physically demanding sport. Depending on the disability, fitness level, or type of snow and terrain, many students need assistance on flats and hills. To aid in forward propulsion, the volunteer may wear a belt with a shock-corded line or rigid poles attached to the frame with a carabiner. Once attached, the volunteer skis or walks in front of the student while assisting in forward propulsion. A student who is fairly fit and independent may need help only occasionally. As an alternative to attaching themselves to the frame, volunteers put a pole tip in the center of the back of the frame and give a push as needed. To help control speed and stop the sit-ski, a 1-inch tubular webbing tether system is

available at the back of the frame. Use a tether or find another route whenever you have any doubt about the student's ability to handle the terrain independently.

Miscellaneous

Before heading out on the trail, whether for an hour or much longer, be sure to bring the following:

- Water for student and volunteer
- Snacks for student and volunteer
- A pack with extra clothing
- Sunscreen and lip balm
- Sunglasses
- Wrench for binding adjustments
- Trail map
- Tether system (even for strong skiers, in case of a broken pole or injury).
- Adjustable pole (in case one is damaged and unusable)
- Radio (for longer trips to check in with base camp)
- Warm footwear

This checklist applies to stand-up skiers as well as sit-skiers.

TEACHING INFORMATION
Introducing the Equipment

Before fitting students into a sit-ski be sure to do the following:

- Explain functional aspects of the sit-ski, poles, and other devices and the importance of layering and hydration.
- Demonstrate how the seat and straps hold the skier snugly and securely.
- Emphasize the importance of a fit that is comfortable and avoids abrasions or pressure injuries.
- Explain the purpose of the fore-and-aft tethering system and model their uses.

- Demonstrate the use of the poles and proper grip adjustment. Show how to change them from a propulsion position to a braking and turning position.
- Introduce safe falling technique and demonstrate how to get up with help and unassisted.
- Review stopping in a hurry. If a hazard lies ahead that cannot be negotiated, yell "fall down," and have the student fall feet first to avoid a head injury.
- Have a plan for transferring the student to and from the sit ski.

Flatland Drills
- Teach how to move about in a perfectly flat area with minimal skier traffic.
- Help the student become familiar with the equipment and learn practical methods for balancing and moving around on flat snow.
- Demonstrate how to push forward using double poling and diagonal poling techniques (watch for "A-framing"—keep the poles parallel to the rig).
- Demonstrate how to push backward by placing the pole tips forward of them and angled toward the foot tray.
- Teach the student to lean from side to side using hands and/or poles for support.
- Teach how to turn by skidding the sit-ski in a circle.
- Demonstrate hop turns—small lifts or "pops" to lift and turn the whole sit-ski (i.e., the student extends quickly from a slouched position, which lifts the chair).

- Help the student achieve an athletic stance that is skeletally aligned, slightly flexed, and balanced with the poles in a parallel position.
- Let the student become familiar with braking on slight declines using hands or pole grips and by putting pressure on the pole baskets and tips.
- Teach various methods of steering the sit-ski using grip/hand placement, weight shift, and pole push-off.
- Show how to get up after a fall.

Adaptive Techniques and Exercises
- Work on body position and balance by placing the poles or hands on the snow and then at the sides. Relax the arms and keep the elbows unlocked, shoulders relaxed, head up, and eyes forward. Rock back and forth from one ski to the other, rotating the upper body left and right and swinging the arms forward and back in opposition.
- Practice falling and getting up. Explain to the student to not try

to break a fall. After falling, the student's poles are placed uphill with the sit-ski across the fall line. The instructor places the uphill ski/boot against the sit-ski and pulls it into an upright position.
- To get up unassisted, the student places the sit-ski across the fall line with both poles uphill. The uphill hand is placed close to the body and pushes off the snow. The downhill pole is pressed against the torso and is at a 45° angle to provide leverage. Pushing with pole and hand brings the sit-ski to an upright position.

Teaching Progression
- Familiarize the student with the equipment and how to achieve and maintain balance (see photo 13.3).
- Evaluate the student's strength, range of motion, balance, cognitive abilities, medications, and ability to feel pressure or cold (see Chapter 2).
- Emphasize proper fit for comfort, security, and performance, with adjustments as necessary to refine the fit.

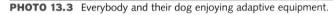

PHOTO 13.3 Everybody and their dog enjoying adaptive equipment.

Courtesy of Michael Byxbe

PHOTO 13.4

Courtesy of Michael Byxbe

- Explore fore-aft and side-to-side balancing movements. Have the student plant the poles evenly with the knees and with arms slightly bent. The student then collapses the body onto the poles, which propels the sit-ski forward. The hands then move back toward and past the hips and return to the starting position with the body upright again. Have the student do the following:
  - ▶ Move forward and backward, like the "hands of a clock" starting with tips and then tails. Have the student move laterally, both left and right.
  - ▶ Tip over (fall) and practice getting up, both assisted and unassisted.
  - ▶ Push forward and glide to a stop.
  - ▶ Push forward, glide, and drag both hands or poles to come to a stop.

- Introduce gliding, propulsion, and direction change. The goal is rhythmic flow of movement and ability to change direction.
- Poles next to hips
  - ▶ center of mass stays centered
  - ▶ short little pushes
  - ▶ good for climbing hills
  - ▶ helps keep from sliding backwards
- Poles between knees and hips
  - ▶ poles reach (bend at waist, shoulders come forward), then come back to hips with a push
  - ▶ poles lifted, brought parallel to rig, then return to reach position
  - ▶ center of mass moves forward by bending at waist and bringing shoulders forward, then returns to center or over hips when push is completed
  - ▶ good when traveling on flat or up gentle hills
- Have the student aim to establish a rhythm. This develops flow, good pacing, and retention of speed.
- With hand or pole, pressure snow to create differential friction and turn rig. To change direction or avoid sliding down a side hill, drag hand on the side toward the direction of intended travel and use the opposite pole to stab out laterally. This will help the sit-ski turn or avoid sliding.
- Body will be slightly tilted in the direction of the turn, with a slight bend at the waist.

- Tethers provide a variety of useful features. They assist in control and provide security for student, can be used to control speed, and can be used pull the student uphill. Gently tightening tether tension either left or right assists in directional change. All tethering movements should be gentle and gradual.

Helpful Hints
- Make sure the skis are waxed for less friction.
- Focus on double and alternate poling.
- Use the "Power U." Arms are positioned flexed and rigid as the student plants the poles to push off.
- Most of the movement comes from the shoulders in a pendulum action. Additional power comes from the elbows during follow-through.
- Tether down hills if needed.
- Coordinate "the crunch" (collapsing of the torso) with the timing of the poles for more body efficiency.

Conclusion
Nordic adaptive track skiing opens new horizons for skiers and will continue to evolve. Although information about adaptive telemark skiing is too sparse to include at the time of publication, it is another area of potential growth for adaptive skiers.

Accessibility at Skiing and Snowboarding Areas

chapter 14

A public entity's services, programs, or activities, when viewed in their entirety, must be readily accessible to and usable by individuals with disabilities. This standard applies to all existing facilities of a public entity. The Americans with Disabilities Act (ADA) and the fact that most snowsports resorts operate on federally owned National Forest land require that both the physical and programmatic aspects of snowsports resorts provide access for people with disabilities. As part of the lease agreement with the U.S. Forest Service, the resort owner/operator agrees to abide by all laws, regulations, and policies of the federal government.

Title II of the ADA prohibits state and local governments from discriminating against persons with disabilities or from excluding their participation in or denying them benefits of services, programs, or activities. It states that a public entity must reasonably modify its policies, practices, or procedures to avoid this type of discrimination. Additionally, Section 504 of Title V of the Rehabilitation Act of 1973 prohibits discrimination against qualified persons with disabilities in the programs or activities of any organization that receives federal financial assistance—including use of National Forest land for all or part of its operations.

The Architectural and Transportation Barriers Compliance Board (Access Board) is the federal agency responsible for developing accessibility guidelines to ensure that construction of new facilities and modification of existing facilities covered by the ADA are readily accessible to and usable by individuals with disabilities, including both on-mountain and base facilities.

In 1994, the Access Board published advanced notice of proposed rule-making to various types of recreational facilities, including snowsports facilities, that were not previously covered by ADA guidelines. An informal advisory committee was established to draft programmatic guidelines for accessibility collaboration with the U.S. Forest Service.

These guidelines where published in December 2000 in the *Accessibility Guidebook for Ski Areas Operating on Public Lands.* The publication was compiled by Beneficial Designs, Inc., with help from the U.S. Forest Service, Wilderness Inquiry, adaptive sports equipment manufacturers, chairlift manufacturers, area operators, skiers with disabilities, and adaptive sports program directors.

Under the requirements of Title 7, Section 15E of the Code of Federal Regulations, all ski areas must determine the accessibility of their programs and facilities and develop a written transition plan. This transition plan must outline how and when the necessary changes to provide accessibility will be implemented. Whatever programs and facilities are provided to the average skier or snowboarder also must be provided to adaptive skiers and riders. The implications of these changes for your local resort are that persons with disabilities must be provided with the same opportunities to learn to ski and ride as anyone else.

Physical accessibility must be provided from the time people arrive in the parking area, including the access route from the parking area to the built facilities. The built facilities must provide accessibility in all components—i.e., daycare centers, cafeterias, equipment storage areas, locker rooms, and bathrooms—and must meet ADA guidelines.

From a programmatic point of view, the availability of equipment and lessons must match the services provided to others. A ski area that provides lessons must also provide instruction for visually impaired, hearing impaired, and mobility impaired skiers. Adaptive skiers or riders at the intermediate level or higher may be integrated into group lessons with other (non-adaptive) students. Adaptive beginner/novice students normally cannot be integrated into lessons for skiers without disabilities without fundamentally altering the lesson, leading most areas to offer separate programs. Adaptive skiers or riders should be able to request and pay for a lesson at a group rate, even if the area chooses to provide a private adaptive lesson.

Adaptive skiers or riders who are accompanied by a helper do not need a discount, but the helper is an essential part of the disabled person's "equipment" and should be allowed to ski or ride for free. Examples of helpers include guides for the visually impaired, interpreters for the hearing impaired, and lifters for sit-skiers. If a discount is provided to adaptive skiers or riders, proof of disability can be required.

If the resort provides space for a concessionaire to rent equipment, standard adaptive ski or snowboard equipment should also be available. At a minimum, available adaptive equipment should include:

- ski-tip stabilizers
- outriggers
- mono-skis
- bi-skis
- bibs for skiers and guides

Advanced notice is generally required for specific types of adaptive ski or snowboard equipment or instruction. Many adaptive skiers or riders need assistance on the mountain in addition to their adaptive equipment. Resorts should be able to provide adaptive assistance at a reasonable fee with advanced notice, just as with the equipment.

Resorts cannot discriminate against adaptive skiers by requiring them to take ski tests before being allowed on the mountain. However, an adaptive skier or rider must follow all aspects of Your Responsibility Code. Failure to comply with the responsibility code can result in the loss of the lift ticket regardless of the disability.

Snowsports areas without adaptive instructors can have their instructors trained at PSIA/AASI-sanctioned adaptive clinics. At some areas, the adaptive instructors and equipment are integrated into the primary ski school, while other areas have a specific adaptive program that works with or adjacent to the school area to provide instruction and rent adaptive equipment. Resorts can also rent equipment from adaptive ski equipment manufacturers.

Brian W. Robb

References

Companion PSIA-AASI Materials

AASI (American Association of Snowboard Instructors) 1998. *Snowboard Manual.* Lakewood, CO.

AASI 1998. *Snowboard Video.* Lakewood, CO.

PSIA (Professional Ski Instructors of America) 2002. *Alpine Technical Manual.* Lakewood, CO.

PSIA 2002. *Alpine Technical Video.* Lakewood, CO.

PSIA 2001. *Core Concepts.* Lakewood, CO.

PSIA 2001. *Telemark Skiing Video.* Lakewood, CO.

PSIA 2000. *Children's Instruction Handbook.* Lakewood, CO.

PSIA 1997. *Adaptive Manual.* Lakewood, CO.

PSIA 1997. *Children's Instruction Manual.* Lakewood, CO.

PSIA 1996. *Alpine Handbook.* Lakewood, CO.

PSIA 1996. *Alpine Manual.* Lakewood, CO.

PSIA 1996. *Alpine Level I, II, and III Study Guides.* Lakewood, CO.

PSIA 1995. *Nordic Skiing.* Lakewood, CO.

PSIA-Eastern Division (PSIA-E) 2002. *Adaptive Education and Exam Guide, 3rd ed.,* PSIA-E Education Foundation, Albany, NY.

PSIA-E 1997. *Adaptive Snowboarding Guide.* PSIA-E Education Foundation, Albany, NY.

The Professional Skier magazine

The Pro Rider magazine

Vagners, J. 1995. *A Ski Instructor's Guide to the Physics and Biomechanics of Skiing.* Lakewood, CO.

Additional References

American Psychiatric Association (APA) 2000. *Diagnostic and Statistical Manual of Mental Disorders.* APA, Washington, DC.

Beers, M.H. 1999. *The Merck Manual of Diagnosis and Therapy, Centennial Edition.* Merck Research Laboratories, NJ.

Butterworth, R.R., and Flodin, M. 1989. *Signing Made Easy.* Berkeley Publishing Group, New York, NY.

City of New York 2001. *Exercise Your Ability: The Ultimate Guide to Sports and Recreation for People with Disabilities.* New York City, NY.

Eichstaedt, C.B., and Lavay, B.W. 1992. *Physical Activities for Individuals with Mental Retardation, Infancy through Adulthood.* Human Kinetics Books, Champaign, IL.

Hendren, J. *Prescription Drug Use Rising in U.S.* Boston Globe: Aug. 31, 1998

Levy, L. 1989. *Picture Communication Symbols Book II.* Mayer Johnson.

Lippencott, Williams, & Wilkins. 2001. *Professional Guide to Diseases.* Springhouse Publishing Co., Springhouse, PA.

Miller, P.D. 1995. *Fitness Programming and Disability.* Human Kinetics Books, Champaign, IL.

O'Leary, H. 1994. *Bold Tracks.* Cordillera Press, Inc., Evergreen, CO.

Physician's Desk Reference, 57th ed. 2003

Post Foster, E. 1995. *Technical Skills for Alpine Skiing.* Turning Point Ski Foundation, South Hero, VT.

Schmidt, R.A., 1991. *Motor Learning and Performance: From Principles to Practice.* Human Kinetics Books, Champaign, IL.

Sharron, M. 2000. *Health Professional's Drug Guide 2000.* Appleton & Lange, Stamford, CT

Sherrill, C. 1997. *Adapted Physical Activity, Recreation, and Sport: Cross Disciplinary and Lifespan.* Brown and Benchmark.

Thomas, C.L., ed. 1998. *Tabers Cyclopedic Medical Dictionary.* F.A. Davis Co., Philadelphia, PA.

Twardokens, G. 1992. *Universal Ski Techniques: Principles and Practices.* Surprisingly Well, Reno NV.

United States Department of Agriculture: Forest Service. 2000. *Accessiblility Guidebook for Ski Areas Operating on Public Lands.* FS-703.

Winick, P.P. 1990. *Adapted Physical Education and Sport.* Human Kinetics Books, Champaign, IL.

Websites

- www.aasi.org
  American Association of Snowboard Instructors
- www.nsaa.org
  National Ski Areas Association
- www.nsp.org
  National Ski Patrol
- www.psia.org
  Professional Ski Instructors of American
- www.snowlink.com
  SnowSports Industries America

Glossary

abduction
Movement away from the midline.

acquired brain injury (ABI)
Brain damage that is caused by disease.

adduction
Movement toward the midline.

amblyopia
Uncorrectable, poor vision not due to any observable disease.

amputation
Removal of a limb, which may predispose the skier to needing special adaptations in equipment or technique. Common sites for amputation are below knee (BK), above knee (AK), below elbow (BE), and above elbow (BE). Unilateral refers to amputations on the same side of the body. Bilateral can refer to either both arms, both legs, or an arm on one side and a leg on the other. Disarticulation refers to removing the limb at the joint. See *disarticulation*.

aphasia
Inability to understand or utilize words and their meanings. Receptive aphasia refers to inability to understand words, while expressive aphasia describes inability to say words formulated in thought.

arthrogryposis
Condition of having immovable joints.

assessment
The process of evaluating student characteristics to determine how to structure individualized, effective lessons. The instructor collects important clues about each student— emotional makeup, expectations, learning preferences, physical ability, and skiing experience— all of which indicate how the student will receive information and respond to learning. The instructor assesses the student throughout the lesson to ensure synthesis and communication.

attention deficit disorder (ADD)
Neurological syndrome that is usually hereditary. Symptoms include distractibility, short attention span, impulsiveness, hyperactivity, and restlessness that interferes with everyday function.

autism
Neurological disorder, also known as pervasive developmental disorder, defined by a symptoms that include severe problems with communication and behavior.

autonomic dysreflexia (AD)
Potentially life-threatening hypertensive occurrence produced by the body's inability to sense and react to specific stimuli. Symptoms include a feeling of impending doom, flushing of the skin, sweating, blurred vision, and/or a sudden change in the ability to comprehend or communicate.

balancing movements
Muscular actions to maintain equilibrium, or the desired alignment, on skis. These movements are usually divided into two categories: (1) actions that affect fore and aft balance and (2) actions that affect lateral balance. Balancing movements are one of the four basic skiing skills.

bi-skiing
Sit-skiing using a molded seating apparatus mounted on two skis.

bucket assist
Straddling a sit-ski from behind and holding the seat to help direct it.

canting
Adjustments done to ski equipment to modify a skier's normal stance.

cants
Shims inserted between the skis and bindings to compensate for the skier's natural stance and allow the ski to rest flat on the snow.

carved turns
Turns in which the skis travel on edge with a minimum of lateral slipping or skidding. Pure carved turns display clean, long arcs in the snow. In most turns the amount of carving depends on the situation, the equipment, and the skier's ability and intent.

cataracts
Opacities and clouding in the eye's lens, blocking light passage through the eye.

center of mass (CM)
The point at which the mass of the body is concentrated. Positioning the CM over the proper spot on the ski is essential to making turns. Mono-skiers have much less ability to shift their CM forward and backward than stand-up skiers. To maintain balance when making turns, the CM must also be positioned properly on the ski to the left and right.

cerebral palsy (CP)
Disorder resulting from anoxia (insufficient oxygen) before, during, or shortly after birth. Brain damage, leading to impaired voluntary muscular coordination, may result in hypertonic (extremely tensed) or hypotonic (very flaccid) muscle groups, or a combination. Classifications of CP include spastic, characterized by constant muscle contraction; athetoid, characterized by constant, slow, writhing movements of the upper extremities; or dystonic, characterized by extreme muscular rigidity.

cerebrovascular disease
Condition affecting the brain and the blood vessels supplying it.

chest harness
See *shoulder straps*.

christie
A turn in which the skis skid on corresponding edges.

clock system
Relating position on the hill to numbers on a clock face. The reference position is that the skier is always facing 12 o'clock.

cognitive disability
Brain damage affecting the ability to process information, and/or to coordinate and control the body or its movement. Disabilities resulting from organic causes (i.e., caused by injury or trauma) include Alzheimer's disease, Parkinson's disease, Huntington's disease, cerebrovascular disease, and brain tumors. These may be progressive, static, or in remission. Disability can also result from nonorganic causes, such as injury or physical trauma. See also *acquired brain injury* and *traumatic brain injury*.

compression
Absorbing the forces generated in skiing. Stand-up skiers use their knees to compress their bodies as they go over bumps. If they didn't, they'd get a jolt and possibly go airborne. Mono-skiers have to let their shock absorber do the absorbing. Some shock absorbers have adjustable slow/fast compression rates. For example, rolling over a bump would cause a slow compression rate, while hitting an abrupt bump would cause a fast compression rate.

cross-over
Moving the body's center of mass forward and across the skis. The center of mass moves from the inside of one turn to the inside of the next turn.

dampener
A piston with hydraulic fluid on both sides. A tiny hole in the piston limits the rate at which it can move through the fluid. If you remove the spring from a shock absorber, you have a dampener, which controls the rate of compression and rebound. A change in the hole and valve size affects the slow/fast rate of compression and rebound. Some dampeners can't be adjusted.

developmental disability
Condition that interrupts or delays normal growth or development, having onset before age 18, and of indefinite duration. Common conditions include mental retardation, cerebral palsy, autism, epilepsy, and Down's syndrome.

Disabled Sports USA (DSUSA)
Organization established to serve disabled persons, their families, and health professionals, providing programs and information on all aspects of the lives of disabled persons.

disarticulation
Removal of a limb at the joint. Disarticulations include hemipelvectomy (H/P), i.e., half of the pelvis and its corresponding limb, and shoulder disarticulation, i.e., removal of the entire arm at the shoulder joint.

dowel test
Balancing test performed with a skier in a sit-ski balanced over a dowel to determine the best position for the seat on the ski.

Down's syndrome
Chromosomal abnormality exhibiting mental retardation in combination with other birth defects. Physical manifestations include a short neck, joint laxity, oval-shaped eyes, and possibly a short stature.

dual ski
A hybrid between a mono-ski and a bi-ski, using two skis.

dynamic parallel
Turns with more carving than skidding where the ski is used as a tool and its energy from decambering flows from one turn to the next.

dyslexia
Condition characterized by a significant delay in one or more areas of learning. Generally occurs in children of average or above intelligence.

edge-control movements
Movements that increase or decrease edge angles. One of the four basic skills of skiing, edging movements include angulation and inclination.

epilepsy
Disorder characterized by disturbed electrical rhythm of the nervous system and typically manifested by lapses of consciousness and/or seizures. Major types of seizures include grand mal, accompanied by loss of consciousness, rigidity, jerking, and falling; petit mal, with a few seconds of unconsciousness; and psychomotor and focal motor, in which a person may be mentally confused, stagger, perform purposeless movements, have facial twitching, or make unintelligible sounds.

evacuation system
Hardware that allows ski patrollers to evacuate a sit-ski from a chairlift.

exercise
Movement patterns that are broken down into component parts and isolated for skill development. Instructors often combine exercises into a progression.

fall line
The imaginary line, through any single point on the slope, that follows the steepest descent. The fall line is the path on which a ball would roll if it were released down the slope.

fan progression
An exercise in which the skier starts in the fall line and turns away from the fall line. It allows skiers to try turning without having to cross the fall line.

fetal alcohol syndrome (FAS)
Disorder found in infants of alcoholic mothers. Characterized by small size and weight before and after birth, small head size, small eyes, underdeveloped upper lip, and impaired brain function manifested by delay in development or intellect. Common behaviors include extreme activity, easy distraction, and impulsiveness.

foot tray
Platform on a sit-ski that secures and protects the lower legs and feet.

fore-and-aft adjustment
The most important adjustment feature on a mono-ski. Programs should look for mono-skis with fore/aft adjustments in increments that will accommodate a variety of body shapes and sizes. Stand-up skiers can shift their center of mass fore and aft over the ski in a much broader range than mono-skiers. A person with T10 paraplegia may only have a total range of 12.5 cm (about 5 in.), while a stand-up skier can normally shift 32 cm (12.6 in.). It is also important to know how easily the adjustment can be made and readjusted on the ski slope.

four-track skiing
Skiing on two skis while using outriggers or a walker for stability.

fragile-X syndrome
Chromosomal abnormality with symptoms that are cognitive, such as mental impairment, attention deficit, hyperactivity, anxiety, and unstable moods; physical, such as a long face, large ears, flat feet, and hyperextensible joints; emotional; and behavioral.

Friedreich's ataxia
Hereditary disease appearing in childhood, involving steady, progressive degeneration of the spinal column and cerebrum. Symptoms include clumsy, uncoordinated movements and muscle imbalance, constriction of some tendons, and possibly scoliosis.

garland
Performing the beginning and end of a series of turns, without the middle of the turn. This linked series takes the skier across the slope without crossing the fall line.

genetic disorders
Conditions resulting from chromosomal abnormalities.

glaucoma
Increased intraocular (inside-the-eye) pressure, which may result in impaired vision or blindness.

grid system
Describing ski runs and terrain for visually impaired skiers by breaking up a distance into imaginary units (e.g., for a run that is "10 across," with a width of 20 yards, a skier can turn at "1 to 5" to make a turn of 10 yards or less).

Guillain-Barre syndrome
Disease of the peripheral nervous system affecting entire nervous system except for brain and spinal cord. Symptoms range from muscle weakness to partial or total paralysis. Also known as polyradiculitis.

handlebar
Attachment to a bi-ski that the skier may grasp.

heel and toe lifts
Materials inserted into boots to bring a skier's center of mass over the center of the foot. Heel lifts shift the center of mass forward and toe lifts shift it aft.

hemiparesis
Partial loss of function or control of one side of the body.

hemiplegia
Complete loss of function or control of one side of the body.

hip check
Forcefully tilting the pelvis during a turn to project a sit-ski down the hill and land on a set edge.

hip projection
Driving the outside hip forward to enable turning in a sit-ski. The motion may be either jerky or smooth.

horse and buggy
Guiding a visually impaired skier by holding one prop (such as a bamboo pole) in each hand while the skier, who is either directly behind or directly in front, holds the opposite ends of the prop at hip level.

Huntington's disease
Hereditary brain disease involving progressive degeneration and shrinkage of brain tissue, especially the basal ganglia. It is characterized by abrupt, jerky, uncontrollable movements that increase during stress or physical exertion.

hypertension
High blood pressure.

inclinometer
A tool used for lateral adjustment of center of mass and measurement of left/right angulation for canting in setting up a mono-ski.

knee bar
Attachment to the suspension system of a sit-ski that provides support under the knees and protects the legs from hyperextension.

lability
Undergoing sudden emotional change in the absence of appropriate stimulus.

learning partnership
The rapport the instructor forms with the student. Essential to the success of this relationship is the instructor's understanding of the student's needs and expectations and the student's willingness to actively participate in learning.

lift-loading mechanism
System of levers and swing arms that mechanically raise a sit-ski into a position suitable for loading onto the chairlift.

linkage
Apparatus that connects the seat of the sit-ski to the ski.

mental retardation
Below-average intellectual ability present from birth or early infancy and associated with difficulties in learning and social adaptation. Classifications include:
- mild (IQ ranging between 51 and 70)
- moderate (IQ ranging between 36 and 50)
- severe (IQ ranging between 21 and 35)
- profound (IQ of 20 or less).

midcord
The middle of the ski, which is determined by measuring the straight-line distance from the tail to the tip of the ski and dividing this distance in half, then measuring that distance from the tail of the ski. For adjusting the ski position it's important to know the desired midcord position of the ski relative to the mono-ski or bi-ski frame.

mono-board
Double-width ski, shorter than a regular ski, with two bindings mounted side by side. Although not designed as an adaptive skiing tool, mono-boards are well-suited to some four-track skiers. A snowboard attached to a bucket is also referred to as a mono-board.

mono-skiing
Sit-skiing using a molded seating apparatus mounted to one ski.

mounting plates
Mounting plates are used to attach the mono and bi-skis to the skis. Many ski manufacturers are now using standard bindings to attach the mono-ski to the ski.

multiple sclerosis (MS)
Neurological disorder in which the body's nerve fibers undergo degeneration and become scarred, or sclerosed. Symptoms may include paralysis or weakness in extremities, loss of stamina, poor balance, incontinence, visual impairment, slurred speech, and/or lability.

muscular dystrophy (MD)
Any of several disorders characterized by progressive and irreversible wasting of muscle tissue, in which the tissue degeneration originates in the muscle itself. Voluntary and involuntary muscles are affected and the person may walk with crutches or a cane, or be confined to a wheelchair.

myopia
Near-sightedness, often caused by the eye being too long from front to back.

non-corrective canting
Adjustments done inside a boot to improve fit or support the feet and legs, without modifying a skier's normal stance. This is used to compensate for leg-length differences, pronation, supination, and to adjust for loose-fitting boots.

nystagmus
Rapid, involuntary oscillation of the eyeballs.

orthosis
A device that assists body functioning by providing external bracing or support to limit or improve the range of motion.

outrigger
Similar to a ski pole with an adapter that allows a ski tip to be attached to the end. The ski tip is retractable and can flip up to expose metal claws for gripping snow (i.e., crutch position). A common outrigger style is a forearm-fitting, Canadian-style crutch. Fixed outriggers can be attached to sit-skis for added stability.

parallel turn
A turn made on corresponding ski edges. It may be more or less carved, depending on the skier's intention and skill.

paraplegia
Paralysis or paresis of the lower half of the body with involvement of both legs.

paresis
Partial paralysis.

physical assists
Helping a student generate movement, or control speed or turning by physically maneuvering the skier's equipment or guiding the skier's body.

plumb bob
Assessment technique that compares the center line of the knee with the boot's center line so boot fitting can be performed to correct misalignment.

post-polio
After-effects of poliomyelitis, a viral infection of the spinal cord that may cause either broadly-distributed or local paralysis. Years after the initial paralysis, the person may exhibit fatigue, shortness of breath, and balance problems.

pressure-control movements
Movements that create, maintain, reduce, or redirect the pressure of the skis on the snow. Pressure control is one of the four fundamental skiing skills. It is achieved through leverage, extension, flexion, and transfer of pressure from ski to ski, all in combination with edge-control movements. Skier movements, ski characteristics, turn shape, terrain, and snow conditions determine the pressure along the ski at any instant.

prosthesis
Artificial device that replaces a missing part of the body.

quadriplegia
Paralysis or paresis of both arms and both legs.

reins
Lengths of 1-inch webbing with clasps on one end. Used from behind the student to help control speed and turns or used in front to pull the student.

retention strap
Strong piece of webbing attached to a sit-ski to keep it firmly attached to the chair.

rotary movements
Movements that increase, limit, or decrease the rotation of the skis. One of the four basic skills, rotary movements can be grouped into four primary categories: (1) rotation, (2) counter-rotation, (3) anticipation release, and (4) rotary push-off.

scoliosis
Lateral curvature of the spine.

seating orthosis
Most of the top US mono-skiers use a customized seating orthosis. To have an orthosis made, it is important to be familiar with many different mono-skis, to determine the most functional body position for skiing. Knowing where to place the feet, knees, pelvis, and upper body position over the mono-ski is crucial. Ideally, a mock-up of the support structure or better yet, sitting in the mono-ski during the plaster splinting process will help to get the best fit. A well-cast mold can also be used to make seats for racing wheelchairs, kayaking, cross-country skiing, etc.

self-loading lift mechanism
Used to raise the mono-ski from skiing height to chairlift loading height.

shock absorber
The shock absorber, which comes in a variety of lengths and ranges of travel, consists of the hydraulic dampener and a spring. "Travel" is the distance the shock moves from full extension to full compression.

shoulder straps or chest harness
Adapts the seating system to support the torso without overly limiting movement. For people with higher SCI lesions who cannot control lateral stability. Students with SCI at T10 and above have successfully used rubber inner tubes and fiberglass spring rods to extend the seat back and give them upper body support. A chest harness made with stretchy bungee or inner tube material can also provide stability, and some harnesses interface with single and double flexible fiberglass rods behind the spine, allowing a user to flex forward and to the side, and then spring to an upright position.

sideslipping
A method of moving down the hill with the skis perpendicular (or across) the fall line.

side step
A method of moving up the hill. With skis across the fall line, the skier steps up sideways, one ski at a time.

sit-skiing
Skiing using equipment that allows the skier to sit. The three types of sit-skiing are a sit-ski (similar to a sled, with metal runners and a slippery plastic bottom), mono-ski, and bi-ski. See also *mono-ski* and *bi-ski*.

ski bra
Metal device that clamps onto the ski tips to keep them together. A "trombone" ski bra is used to keep skis parallel.

skill
The capability to bring about a result with maximum certainty, minimum energy, or minimum time.

skills concept
The four fundamental skiing skills: balancing, rotary, edge-control, and pressure-control movements. The skills concept, which is an essential aspect of PSIA and AASI's teaching system, provides instructors a base from which to evaluate, prioritize, and develop student performance.

slant board
Board mounted between the ski and binding, used to slant the skier fore, aft, or laterally, or to compensate for gross leg-length difference.

socket and suspension system
Method for affixing a prosthesis to the body in a way that will prevent it from slipping, turning, or causing friction during use.

spacer bar
Hollow piece of tubing through which a bungee cord is threaded and knotted at the ends. The bar stretches across the bindings and attaches on the lateral side of the ski boots to provide lateral support.

spina bifida (SB)
Congenital malformation of the spinal column in which segments of the spine fail to fuse, allowing the spinal cord to protrude. A surgically implanted shunt or tube may be necessary to allow cerebrospinal fluid to drain. Scoliosis may be present.

spinal cord injury (SCI)
Trauma to the spinal cord, resulting in partial or full loss of function and sensation below the injury level, possibly resulting in paraplegia or quadriplegia. See also *paraplegia* and *quadriplegia*.

spring
The spring on many shock absorbers is removable. Variable spring rates are available; a softer spring works better on a downhill course, and stiffer springs are better on a slalom course.

stance
How a skier stands on skis. One of the most basic indicators of performance at all levels of skiing, stance affects the application and blending of skills.

strabismus
Eyes muscles not working properly, resulting in eyes not facing the same direction, and perhaps double vision. Also known as eye turn.

straight lifts
Materials added to the boot liner to compensate for leg-length difference.

straight run
Skiing directly down the fall line with the skis in a parallel relationship. Also called schussing (German).

stroke
Sudden weakness or other neurologic symptom resulting from injury to a blood vessel in the brain. Also referred to as a cerebrovascular accident (CVA).

suspension
One feature of a sit-ski, this acts as a shock absorber and helps to keep the ski in contact with the snow.

suspension linkage
The configuration of suspension linkage determines the path of movement the skier's center of mass will take from full compression to full rebound. A scissor-type mechanism allows only vertical movement, as does a single-pivot linkage. Four-bar linkages may have short or long bars; the longer bars will likely result in less forward displacement, depending on their angle. For safety reasons, any suspension that only moves part of the body should not be used. Note that the position and orientation of the shock absorber has nothing to do with the relative path of the mechanism's movement.

t-bar hardware
A device to use with the T-bar, consider the best attachment point to the mono-ski. Pull in front of and slightly above the skier's center of mass. Be sure to have a good release system.

tether
Device used to help control the student's speed and turn shape. This consists of two pieces of line, 18 to 20 feet long, with carabiners or a hook attached to one end. One end is held and the other is clipped to the student's ski bra, binding, walker, or harness.

three-track skiing
Skiing on one ski while using outriggers to maintain balance.

thousand steps
Stepping through a parallel turn using a number of quick, small steps.

thumpers
Skiing in a traverse while lifting one ski up and placing it back down on the snow repeatedly.

tip hold
Maneuver in which the instructor skis backwards, holding the tips of the adaptive skier's skis.

traumatic brain injury (TBI)
Brain damage resulting from either organic causes (i.e., disease) or inorganic causes (i.e., trauma). May affect almost any aspect of movement, thought, or behavior. Hemiplegia, hemiparesis, lability, memory loss, aphasia, and/or seizures are commonly associated with TBI.

two-point hold
Physical assist in which the instructor's skis are inserted between student's two skis. The instructor places one hand on the student's hip and one hand on the outside knee. When making a right turn, pressure is applied to the student's left knee and, if necessary, the right hip is gently pulled back. This assists rotary movement needed to initiate the turn. Hands and head position can be switched or remain the same for the next turn. Shorter skis are helpful for this type of assist.

visual impairment
Disability involving reduction or loss of vision, usually described in terms of acuity or range. Classifications include legal blindness, partial sightedness, or total blindness.

walker
In adaptive skiing, this refers to a walker mounted on skis. The is a type of four-track skiing.

wedge-christie turn
A turn that begins with opposing edges (in a wedge) and finishes with a skidding phase, resulting in corresponding edges (in a parallel). See also *christie* and *wedge turn*.

wedge turn
A turn with skis in a converging (wedge) position, with the skier maintaining opposing edges throughout the turn.

Your Responsibility Code
A code that sets forth the responsibility of each participant for safe conduct on the ski slopes and lifts. There are seven points to the code. It is meant to be a partial list of safe conduct with the message to always be safety conscious. This code is endorsed by NSAA, NSP, and PSIA-AASI.

Index